Downloading Copyrighted Stuff From the Internet
Stealing or Fair Use?

ISSUES IN FOCUS TODAY

Sherri Mabry Gordon

Enslow Publishers, Inc.

40 Industrial Road   PO Box 38
Box 398   Aldershot
Berkeley Heights, NJ 07922   Hants GU12 6BP
USA   UK

http://www.enslow.com

Library of Congress Cataloging-in-Publication Data

Gordon, Sherri Mabry.
    Downloading copyrighted stuff from the Internet : stealing or fair use? / Sherri
Mabry Gordon.
        p. cm. — (Issues in focus)
    Includes bibliographical references and index.
    ISBN 0-7660-2164-5
    1. Copyright—Electronic information sources—United States—Juvenile literature.
2. Internet—Law and legislation—United States—Juvenile literature. 3. Piracy
(Copyright)—United States—Juvenile literature. 4. Copyright—Music—United
States—Juvenile literature. I. Title. II. Issues in focus today (Berkeley Heights, N.J.)
    KF3024.C6G67 2005
    346.7304'82—dc22

                                                            2004009954

Printed in the United States of America

10 9 8 7 6 5 4 3 2 1

To Our Readers:
We have done our best to make sure all Internet Addresses in this book were active and
appropriate when we went to press. However, the author and the publisher have no control over and assume no liability for the material available on those Internet sites or on
other Web sites they may link to. Any comments or suggestions can be sent by e-mail to
comments@enslow.com or to the address on the back cover.

Illustration Credits: AP/Wide World, pp. 3, 18, 61, 69; Corbis Images Royalty-Free, pp. 3,
28, 80; Enslow Publishers, Inc., pp. 20, 22, 24; EyeWire Images, p. 8; Hemera Image
Express, pp. 3, 5, 15, 32, 37, 65, 74, 87; istockphoto.com, pp. 1, 3, 11, 26, 46, 91, 93;
Photos.com, pp. 3, 14, 29, 39, 50, 53, 57, 66, 77, 89, 95.

Cover Illustration: istockphoto.com.

Contents

346.7304 GOR

D1698822X

Acknowledgments

The author would like to acknowledge
Dave Dulany of Aurora University
and
Mark Ishikawa, CEO of BayTSP,
for their comments,
and to give
special thanks to her husband,
Peter J. Gordon, for all his help
on the manuscript.

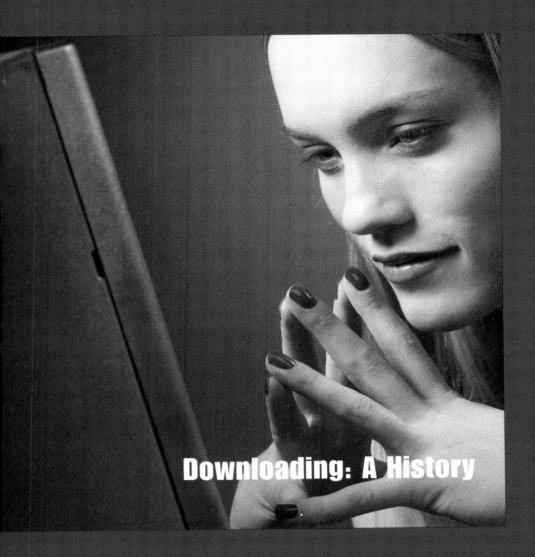

Downloading: A History

Melody is a bright, energetic 18-year-old college student with an interest in architecture, a thirst for music, and a love of the Internet. Like most teenagers, Melody uses the Internet primarily for research and learning, keeping in touch with family members, chatting with friends, buying concert tickets, and playing online games.

"Kids my age are truly the Internet Age," she says. "Without the Internet, I don't think we'd know what to do. We can find anything, do anything online with a matter of a few clicks."[1]

Melody (not her real name) also uses the Internet to download music, movies, video clips, and software programs.

Her collection is mostly music, about three thousand songs, and growing. Sharing music online is a particularly popular pastime for teenagers like Melody.

Using peer-to-peer file-sharing programs on the Internet, young people search for and download all kinds of music, including tunes by everyone from Avril Lavigne and No Doubt to Ani Di Franco and the Dave Matthews Band. The options are endless.

This use of the Internet to download copyrighted material without paying for it is sometimes referred to as "the underground Internet."

In July 2003, the Pew Internet and American Life Project reported that 29 percent of Internet users (about 35 million American adults) have "downloaded music files to their computer so they can play them anytime they want." What's more, 67 percent of those who do download music files say they do not care whether the files are copyrighted or not.[2]

A copyright is a form of protection provided by the laws of the United States to the person or organization that created the material. Copyrighted material includes music, movies, books, software programs, computer games, photographs, newspaper and magazine articles, radio and television programs, and works of art.

The study found that Americans aged eighteen to twenty-nine are less likely to be concerned about copyright than any other age group, and that students are more likely to download music than non-students. Fifty-six percent of full-time students and 40 percent of part-time students report downloading music files.[3]

"[Downloading music is] more convenient and cheaper—and that's important when you're in college—than going out to the record store and spending twenty dollars on a CD when you may only want one or two songs off the CD," Melody says.[4]

But the music industry does not view this type of file sharing as a harmless pastime. They claim to have lost millions of dollars due to online music swapping. As a result, there is a major debate over the legality of online file sharing.

"Finding your favorite song online has become as easy as checking the weather or the latest sports scores," says Lee Rainie, director of the Pew Internet and American Life Project. "Millions of Americans have joined the online music revolution in recent months. . . . It's a huge threat to the music industry now and it is an [indication] of the trouble the Internet will pose to other entertainment forms like the movies."[5]

What Is Peer-to-Peer File Sharing?

Peer-to-peer, or p2p, is technology that allows people to share files and information. The most popular information swapped through p2p technology is music, movies, and software. However, there is no limit to the types of information that can be shared.

In simple terms, peer-to-peer technology allows two or more devices, such as personal computers, to share files and information through the Internet. When using a peer-to-peer network, people can request information, offer information, or do both. The person who requests information is called a client, and the person who offers information is called a server. The person who acts as both a server and a client at the same time is called a servent (**serv**er + cli**ent**).

Using p2p technology to share information and files became extremely popular in the late 1990s when a company called Napster began offering its music-swapping service. Soon it became one of the most widely used p2p applications on the Internet. (An application is any program designed to perform a specific function.) In February 2001, Napster said it had an average of 1.57 million simultaneous users per day until a court decision shut it down.[6] Since then, numerous programs have popped up to try to fill the file-trading void. Some of these

Teens today can find anything, do anything online with a few clicks of the mouse.

programs include LimeWire, which uses the Gnutella network, and Kazaa, which uses the FastTrack network.

History of P2P

Peer-to-peer technology is not a new idea, even though the general public did not begin using the technology until the 1990s. Sharing information through a network of computers was first done with computerized bulletin board systems (BBSs). The first BBS was a message-posting network that was created by Ward Christensen and Randy Seuss in the late 1970s.[7]

A BBS worked a lot like a thumbtack bulletin board—except that it was computerized. After dialing in, people posted messages to a public "board." Other people then read and responded to those messages. After an article explaining BBSs was published in 1978, many people and organizations began developing their own systems.[8]

The Difference Between the Internet and the World Wide Web

Many people believe that the Internet and the World Wide Web (also called the Web) are the same thing. In fact, the Internet and the Web are two different but related things.

The Internet is a massive network that connects millions of computers together around the world. Through this network, any computer can communicate with any other computer as long as they are both connected to the Internet. Information that travels over the Internet does so through a variety of languages known as protocols.

The Web is a way of accessing information over the Internet. It is an information-sharing model that is built on top of the Internet. The Web uses hyptertext transfer protocol, or HTTP—only one of the languages used over the Internet—to transmit data. The Web also uses browsers, such as Internet Explorer or Netscape, to access Web pages.

The Web is just one of the ways that information can be distributed over the Internet. E-mail is another example. Although the Web is a very large portion of the Internet, it is not the same thing.

By the early 1990s most BBSs were connected to the Internet. There were more than 60,000 BBSs in the United States alone.[9] Then, as the World Wide Web became more popular, membership in BBSs began to decrease. Soon people were surfing the Web to get the information they needed.

File Sharing and Piracy

While the original intent of BBSs and most other file-sharing methods was for good purposes, not all file sharing today is on the up-and-up or even legal. The vast majority of file sharing is in the form of online computer piracy. If something is pirated, it is copied without permission from the owner or copyright holder.

By law, only copyright owners can make copies or reproduce copyrighted material. Only they can give permission to others to copy the material or use it in another way. Making copies of copyrighted material without permission from the owner is against the law. Unfortunately, most of the files shared using peer-to-peer technology are copyrighted and should not be copied without permission.

Although there are many types of computer piracy, there are three main areas in which copyrights are violated online. These areas are music piracy, software piracy, and movie piracy.

Music Piracy

Music is widely available online in a digital format called MP3 (short for MPEG-1 Layer 3). Using MP3 to pirate music is relatively new. MP3s allow people to compress music files without affecting the quality of the sound.

A file that is compressed is smaller in size and takes up less space on a CD. As a result, pirates can leave songs compressed and fit more than ten hours of music on a CD that will play through their computer. What's more, devices similar to the

Sony Walkman have been created that will play MP3 compressed files.

Although MP3 technology is not illegal, trading pirated copies of music in an MP3 format is. On the Internet there are many Web sites and online groups devoted to MP3 file sharing. Not all MP3s online are pirated copies, but many are. MP3 file sharing is one of the busiest areas for teens online today.

Software Piracy

Pirates today have exploited just about every type of software, from video games to home software to business applications. You can find just about anything online. Pirated software, or software that is copied without permission, is often called "warez." Warez is a slang term widely used by people who trade pirated software.

Talented computer programmers known as "crackers" can break the protection codes on software. Then, they post the software online in what are called "cracked" copies. These copies can be downloaded and used without the need for a registration number. However, pirated software also may contain bugs and

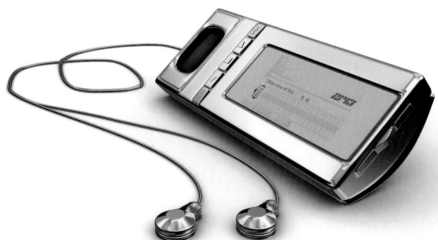

The invention of the MP3 player enabled people to play compressed music files without losing high-quality sound.

other flaws that could harm the material on a person's computer. Using pirated software can increase your risk of infecting your computer with a virus.

The most popular way to get warez is through the Internet. Many people use file-sharing services to get pirated software. Because the Internet is growing, connections are getting faster, and technology is improving, software piracy is growing quickly. Pirated copies of software can be downloaded quickly all around the world at the click of a mouse. In the long run, though, the use of pirated software hurts everyone. Software companies often increase prices to make up for losses due to piracy.

Movie Piracy

A few years ago, downloading a movie took days and maybe even weeks. Now, with high-speed Internet connections in many homes and the ability to compress a movie's size, it takes only a short time to download a full movie. The invention of DVDs has made it much easier to transfer videos to the computer with pretty good quality.

To trade movies online, people often use downloadable media formats, digital files that allow movies to be compressed—much like compressing music using MP3 technology. Afterwards, this compressed version can be downloaded onto a computer and later traded or shared through file-sharing services.

Another common way that movies are pirated over the Internet is through circumvention devices. A circumvention device is used to break copy protection on DVDs. This practice makes it possible for movies on DVDs to be decrypted, or converted to an unprotected version. Later, this DVD can be copied onto a computer's hard drive and shared illegally over the Internet—in perfect digital format. As a result of piracy like this, the U.S. motion picture industry claims to suffer staggering losses each year.

Peer-to-Peer Piracy on University Campuses

More than 2.6 billion music files are illegally downloaded every month on peer-to-peer file-sharing systems.[10] Much of this traffic occurs on college campuses around the country.

The reason is simple. Colleges and universities typically have fast Internet connections, which make downloading files a quick process. Plus, most college kids are technically savvy and do not have a lot of money. Add it all together and you can see why college students do most of the file sharing.

Many times the campus computer networks are used instead of the Internet to pirate material. Some students have developed Napster-like systems on university campuses so that students can copy each other's files within the university network.[11] By doing so, downloading files can take place even more quickly and easily than downloading from the Internet.

To combat this growing problem, the copyright industries and university leaders have joined together to form the Joint Committee of the Higher Education and Entertainment Communities.[12]

P2P Users Get a Warning

Beginning in April 2003, a music industry organization, the Recording Industry Association of America (RIAA), began using the instant messaging (IM) function of certain peer-to-peer networks to let users know that offering copyrighted music on those networks is illegal and that they could face punishment when they participate in this illegal activity.[13]

The instant message campaign also is designed to let users know that they are not anonymous when they use file-sharing services.

"Unfortunately, many users of systems like Kazaa and Grokster may be under the mistaken impression that anything they do on these systems is now legal," says Cary Sherman of the RIAA. "In fact, every court decision regarding peer-to-peer

While many teens view online file sharing as harmless, copyright holders do not see it that way.

networks has confirmed that distributing or downloading copyrighted music without permission of the copyright owner is illegal. And that's the message we want to get across to users of these systems."[14]

The campaign also will let users know about other risks, such as exposing their computers and private files to anyone on the Internet. The RIAA says they hope the campaign will educate users and encourage them to stop stealing music.

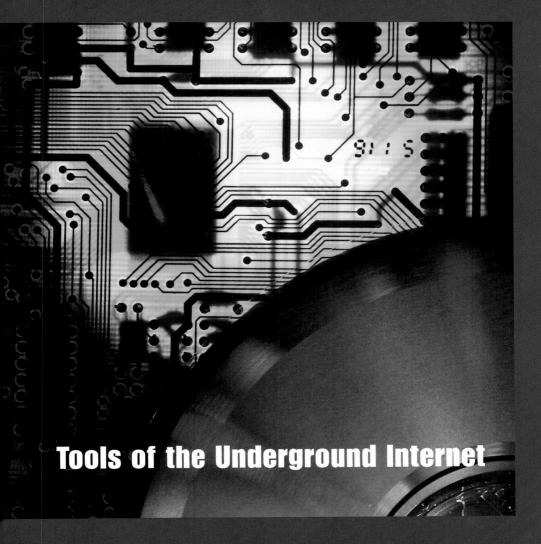

Tools of the Underground Internet

When his college roommate could not find the MP3s he was looking for online, 19-year-old Shawn Fanning had a brainstorm. What if he created a program that allowed people to share MP3 files? Instead of making music fans hunt down the songs they wanted from various Web sites, Fanning, a computer science student, would build a program that let users share tunes one-to-one.

The result was a company called Napster. The name came from a nickname Fanning's friends gave him because his shaggy hair looked a little "nappy." Napster soon became one of the fastest growing Internet companies ever in terms of users.

Just seven months after Fanning quit college and moved to Silicon Valley, Napster's popularity had gone through the roof. Hundreds of thousands of college students and music fans had downloaded the firm's free software. Napster's software allowed users to swap MP3 songs, the Internet's most popular digital music format. Napster's user base grew by as much as 25 percent a day.[1]

The attraction was this: Napster acted like a digital matchmaker, making the search for songs extremely easy. By looking into the users' hard drives and publishing, on a central database, a list of all the songs found, Napster created the Internet's largest music library, without owning or selling any music.

To locate a song, all the user had to do was enter the title or the name of the artist. If anyone else on the network had it, the user could download the tune from that person's computer with a click of a button.

What Shawn Fanning did not count on was how the music industry or the artists would react. To those in the industry, his brilliant idea—which delighted music fans all around the world—was nothing more than a major piracy operation that broke numerous copyright laws and stole money from artists.

In December 1999, the Recording Industry Association of America sued Napster for copyright violations, hoping to shut it down and collect more than $100 million in damages.[2] The RIAA represents a large part of the U.S. recording industry. Moreover, hundreds of colleges and universities started blocking student access to Napster.

In April 2000, Metallica, a heavy metal rock group, became the first band to take legal action against Napster, suing it for copyright infringement. Rapper Dr. Dre filed a suit just two weeks later. Then, in May, Metallica produced a list of more than 335,000 users it said used Napster to transfer its songs illegally.[3]

It was the beginning of a long and heated court battle—a battle that would change Napster forever. Just five months after the RIAA filed its suit, a federal court in San Francisco ruled that Napster was in violation of the Digital Millennium Copyright Act (DMCA). The court required Napster to shut down by July 2000.[4]

In the meantime, Napster settled its legal disputes with both Dr. Dre and Metallica. Napster agreed to place recordings by the artists on its file-sharing system only if they agreed in advance and if copyright protections were ensured.

By June 2002 Napster had filed for bankruptcy. Then, in September 2002, a judge blocked the sale of Napster to Bertelsmann, an international publishing and entertainment company, due to a conflict of interest problem. It appeared that the days of Napster were officially over. Then, in early 2003, Roxio, a U.S. software maker, announced that it would relaunch the file-sharing company—this time with the music industry's support. To help guarantee this support, Roxio purchased PressPlay in May 2003. PressPlay is a legal digital music distribution system with catalog rights from five major music labels. It served as the foundation for relaunching the new online music service under the Napster name. It is completely legal and is supported by the industry.[5]

"With our acquisition of Napster we obtained the most powerful brand in the online music space," Chris Gorog, Roxio's chairman and CEO, says. "Now with our acquisition of PressPlay, we have the most complete and . . . legal technology . . . to use [to] re-launch Napster."[6] It remains to be seen if Napster can make it as a legitimate file-sharing network.

How Does Peer-to-Peer File Sharing Work?

While Napster caused much of the frenzy over peer-to-peer initially, the current p2p craze is about much more than just swapping music. These fascinating—and sometimes misused— tools offer ways to share just about any kind of information. From movies, music, and software to genealogy facts, auction

Shawn Fanning, founder of Napster, speaks at a news conference in 2001. The podium and background show the Napster logo of a cat wearing headphones.

items, and medical records, the types of information that can be shared is endless. As peer-to-peer technology becomes more and more popular, the number of options for file sharing is increasing.

There are three different types of peer-to-peer file-sharing networks:

- Centralized network (e.g., Napster)

- Decentralized network (e.g., Gnutella)

- Controlled decentralized network (e.g., FastTrack/Kazaa)[7]

These networks determine how each user can find the files they are looking for.

Centralized P2P Network

A centralized peer-to-peer network has a central server that works rather like an air traffic controller, directing the traffic on the network.

The central server keeps lists of the shared files that are stored on each peer (or node). Every time someone logs on or off the network, the server's list is updated with the files that are available. For example, if you have copies of tunes from Avril Lavigne, Norah Jones, No Doubt, and Sheryl Crow saved on your computer, the central server would be updated to include a complete list of your songs. When you sign off, the central server would be updated again. Your list of songs would be removed from the central server's list.

When someone (a client) requests a file, such as a song by Britney Spears, the request is sent to the central server. The server then compares the request with its list and shows the client the matches.

Once the match is seen, the client then connects directly to the peer (the person that has the Britney Spears song) and downloads the file. It is important to remember that the actual file—in this case a song by Britney Spears—is never stored

Centralized P2P Network

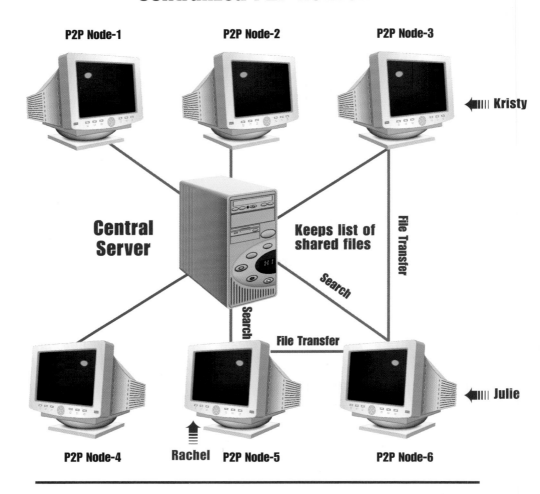

P2P Node-1 **P2P Node-2** **P2P Node-3**

◀IIII **Kristy**

Central Server

Keeps list of shared files

File Transfer

Search

Search

File Transfer

◀IIII **Julie**

P2P Node-4 **Rachel** **P2P Node-5** **P2P Node-6**

Julie asks her Napster service for songs by Avril Lavigne. Her request goes from her PC to Napster's central server. The central server searches its list and sees that Kristy is signed on and has songs by Avril Lavigne as well as Incubus, Ashanti, and OutKast.

The central server shows Julie the match, and she connects directly to Kristy to download the Avril Lavigne tune she wants.

Meanwhile, the central server's list is updated to include Julie's list of songs too. Her list includes tunes by Norah Jones, Guster, Pink, and Phantom Planet. So, when Rachel makes a request for a Norah Jones tune, the central server shows her that Julie has a match. Rachel connects to Julie and downloads the Norah Jones song.

on the central server. The only thing the server keeps is an updated list of what is available from the network's users. The centralized peer-to-peer network is very quick and efficient in locating files.

Decentralized P2P Network

In a decentralized peer-to-peer network, there is no central server, and every peer (or node) has equal status. Each node acts as a servent, which means the node can be both a client (requesting information) and a server (giving information) while on the network.

Every node in the network tries to keep a certain number of connections at all times—usually four to eight—to other nodes. The connected nodes carry the network's communications. These communications are usually made up of requests and answers to those requests.

In order to share files using this network, every user needs a networked computer that has the same file-sharing program.

Because a decentralized network does not have a central server, it can be larger and stronger than a centralized network. However, search times can be a lot longer than with a centralized network. For example, a request may have to go through thousands of users before a match is found. Gnutella uses a decentralized network.

Controlled Decentralized P2P Network

A controlled decentralized peer-to-peer network is a mix between the centralized and decentralized networks. Within the controlled decentralized network, some nodes are selected to be "super nodes."

Usually super nodes are powerful PCs that have fast connections to the Internet. They are selected by the system to help run the network. As a result, a client node (or peer) only has to keep a small number of connections open—including a

Decentralized P2P Network

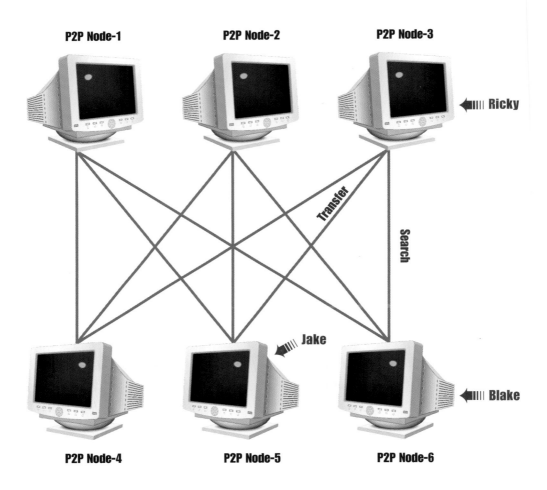

P2P Node-1   **P2P Node-2**   **P2P Node-3**

◀IIII **Ricky**

Transfer

Search

◀IIII **Jake**

◀IIII **Blake**

P2P Node-4   **P2P Node-5**   **P2P Node-6**

Ricky asks his Gnutella service for heavy-metal music files. His request goes from his PC to Blake's PC. The request is passed along to several other Gnutella subscribers as well.

Blake's PC does not have a match. It sees that Ricky's computer is online and requesting heavy-metal files. Blake's PC passes the request to Jake's PC as well as to other PCs.

Jake's PC has files that match Ricky's request. Jake's PC sends match information to Blake's PC, which tells Ricky's PC. Ricky selects the files he wants and downloads them directly from Jake.

connection to a super node. It also reduces the number of nodes involved in receiving and sending messages.

Super nodes allow requests to be answered quickly—much like a centralized network. In the controlled decentralized network, each node forwards a list of its shared files to its super node. FastTrack/Kazaa is an example of a controlled decentralized network.

File-Sharing Network Protocols

The following is a list of file-sharing network protocols. Keep in mind that this list is constantly changing. Because of legal action, some of these network protocols may no longer exist, and newly created network protocols that have become popular since the publication of this book will not be listed.

Gnutella—allows trading of all file types

FastTrack/Kazaa—allows trading of all file types

WinMX/OpenNap—allows trading of all file types

Freenet—allows trading of all file types

Blubster—allows trading of MP3 files only

Edonkey—allows trading of all file types

DirectConnect—allows trading of all file types

File-Sharing Services

File-sharing services are software applications or programs designed to perform a specific job. File-sharing services typically use one type of network protocol. LimeWire is an example of a file-sharing service. LimeWire uses the Gnutella network protocol to allow its users to communicate and share files. Other examples of file-sharing services include Kazaa, Grokster, Morpheus, and BearShare.

Controlled Decentralized Network

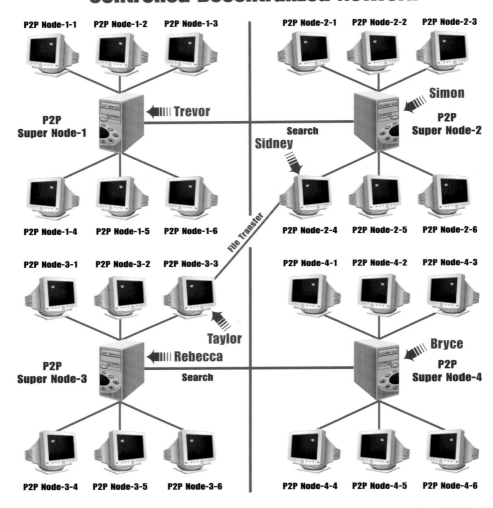

Sidney signs on to her FastTrack service and is assigned to a super node—Simon's PC. Simon's PC has been designated by the network to be a super node because he has a fast connection to the Internet. Sidney forwards a list of her shared songs to Simon. Simon's list of shared files is updated.

Meanwhile, Sidney requests a tune by 3 Doors Down. Simon forwards the request to the other super nodes—Trevor's PC, Bryce's PC, and Rebecca's PC. The other super nodes search their lists to find a match. Rebecca's PC indicates that Taylor—one of the nodes assigned to her—has a match. Simon's PC lets Sidney's PC know where the match is. Sidney connects directly to Taylor to download the song.

A Closer Look at Popular Network Protocols

Gnutella

Gnutella is an extremely popular file-sharing network protocol that was developed by Nullsoft in late 1999. Nullsoft, a subsidiary of America Online (known today as AOL-TimeWarner) was a group of talented computer programmers. These programmers also created the WinAmp MP3 player.

Gnutella hit the Internet in the spring of 2000, but AOL quickly shut it down. Consequently, Nullsoft was no longer able to use the company's money to develop this technology. But the information was already out there and it caught on, because the programming code used to create the system was made available. As a result, people such as developers could use or change the code as they saw fit.

One of biggest differences between Gnutella and Napster is that Gnutella is decentralized and Napster is centralized. Centralized means the technology uses a central server. Decentralized means there is no central server. Without a central server, people can search for information and files almost anonymously.

With Gnutella, users connect directly to one another anonymously and not to a central server. Because everyone on the network receives the request for a specific song until a match is found, it sometimes can take a long time for a match to be found.

FastTrack/Kazaa

FastTrack's Niklas Zennstrom, an engineer who specializes in telecommunications, created Kazaa. The FastTrack/Kazaa network protocol blends features of both Napster and Gnutella.

FastTrack designates "super nodes" on the network. These super nodes are powerful PCs that have fast connections to the Internet. They are identified by the system to devote a small percentage of their resources to help run the network. Anyone can be selected at random to be a super node. The super nodes hold an index of who has what song and direct requests accordingly. This feature prevents requests from going to every participant, as it would with Gnutella.

DirectConnect

DirectConnect works in a way similar to Kazaa. Users can set up their own "activity centers" with their own restrictions.[8] To get files from DirectConnect, the user first has to pick an activity center from a public list. Most of the activity centers are specialized, meaning if the user wanted to trade music he or she would need to find an activity center on the list that specializes in music.

Because you cannot search more than one activity center at a time, it may take a long time to find a match. DirectConnect can be one of the most complicated file-sharing networks to use.

People who use file-sharing services say it allows them to download only the songs they like rather than paying for an entire CD.

WinMX/OpenNap

Designed by a company called Frontcode Technologies, WinMX first used the peer-to-peer network protocol OpenNap.[9] OpenNap consisted of machines that had popped up all over the world designed to mimic the Napster servers. When Napster was shut down by the courts, most of the OpenNap servers shut down as well.

Today, WinMX can connect you to the few OpenNap servers still around. It has its own network protocol, much like FastTrack's. Additionally, it claims not to install spyware on your machine.

Freenet

Ian Clarke, a computer programmer, created Freenet. He started developing the system in 1998 while attending the University of Edinburgh. Originally, Freenet was designed as a way for dissidents in countries without free speech to have a voice. They could post ideas and information without fear of harm from their governments.[10]

However, Freenet allows anything to be traded or shared on the Internet. Users are likely to see everything from political information to pirated music videos to child pornography. Freenet is open to anyone to freely publish or view information of all kinds.[11]

Freenet does not require its users to sign on or identify themselves. It is decentralized, meaning there is no central server. For this reason, industry experts fighting piracy say Freenet may be the most difficult to fight. They still insist it can be done.

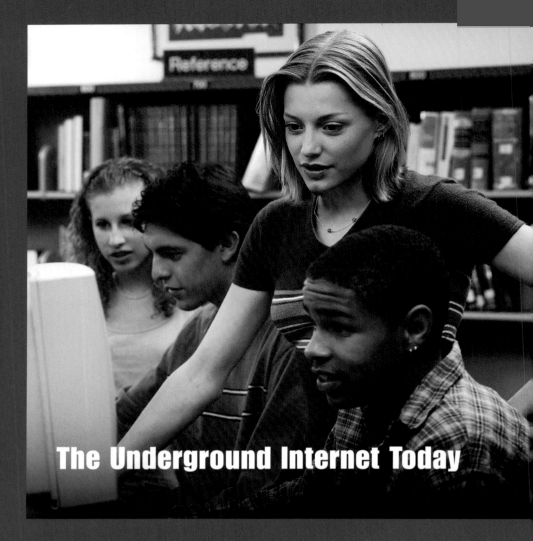

The Underground Internet Today

We live in the Digital Age. The Internet is digital, and so are all the movies, music, and software that are on the Internet.[1] Because of this, it is extremely easy to make copies. Whether you want to find the latest song by Incubus or you need to find a copy of an Austin Powers movie you missed, it usually can be done. It is getting easier by the day.

While it may be easy and fun to find just what you are looking for, unless you already own copies of the material, it is piracy. And piracy is stealing.

Piracy is a huge problem today. Most young people do not realize that downloading files for free—whether it is music, movies, games, or software programs—is illegal. It does not help that many people also think that trading movies, music, computer games, and software online is a very cool thing to do.

Despite efforts to educate the public on the need to respect copyrights, only one out of five downloaders age twelve and older believe that online file sharing hurts artists, and 39 percent of downloaders feel that making copies of music to give to friends is okay.[2]

With piracy, everyone gets hurt. The people involved with piracy can be arrested. The people making the material that is pirated lose money they are entitled to. And the people who do not pirate copyrighted material have to foot the bill for piracy through higher prices for products.

One real-world example of the impact of piracy is the release of *Star Wars: Episode 1—The Phantom Menace.* Pirated copies of the film were made using camcorders in U.S. theaters. Then these copies were distributed in Asia. When the movie opened in Asian theaters, attendance was lower than expected. What is more, home video sales and video rental stores lost money too. Because of piracy, theaters, exhibitors, and local businesses—as well as the people who were involved in writing, producing, directing, and performing in the movie—all lost money that was rightly theirs.[3]

The technological breakthroughs that brought the Digital Age made it very easy to copy material—songs, movies, games, and software.

Overall, the annual losses due to piracy are staggering. For example, the music industry estimates that it loses about $4.2 billion worldwide due to piracy each year.[4]

The movie industry estimates that its losses are more than $3 billion,[5] while the software industry estimates that its losses due to piracy are nearly $11 billion.[6]

Know the Rules: What's Legal and What's Not

The rules are simple when it comes to music, movies, and software that belong to you. The key is that you have to already own a copy—in other words, you purchased or paid for it—to be able to make copies. Here is a summary of what you can do legally:

- You can make a backup copy of any piece of software or CD you own in case your original gets damaged.

- You can transfer any piece of software or CD you own to another format. For example, if you own a Britney Spears CD, you can make an MP3 version of it.[7]

There are a number of things you cannot do with copies of software, CDs, and movies. Here is a summary of what is against the law:

- You cannot give an MP3 version of a CD you own to a friend. Your friend should buy the CD and then make his or her own MP3.

- You cannot download a shareware program from a site online and then neglect to pay for it. Shareware is software that is distributed free on a trial basis with the understanding that if the user decides he needs it later he will pay for it.

- You cannot share your computer software program disks with a friend—even if he or she cannot afford to buy the program.

- You cannot go to a music file-sharing Web site and download a copy of a song from a CD that you do not own.

- You cannot make a copy of your new DVD. DVDs have copy protection built in, and under the Digital Millennium Copyright Act (DMCA) it is illegal to crack the copy protection on a DVD.[8]

What Do the Laws Say?

There are a number of laws that deal with copyrights and online file sharing. Many of these laws are just now being put to the test in court. Aside from the Copyright Act of 1976, the two most important laws are the No Electronic Theft Act (NET Act) and the DMCA.

There are several international laws and entities that are also worth noting. These include the Berne Convention for Protection of Literary and Artistic Works, the World Intellectual Property Organization (WIPO), the Trade Related Aspects of Intellectual Property Rights (TRIPS Agreement), and the World Intellectual Property Organization Copyright Treaty (WCT).

No Electronic Theft Act. In December 1997, President Bill Clinton signed into law a new statute directly aimed at reducing copyright infringement on the Internet.[9] (A statute is a law enacted by a legislative branch of government.) This new law, the No Electronic Theft Act, is nicknamed the NET Act.

The NET Act was passed to close a copyright law loophole. A loophole in the law is a way for someone to avoid punishment. Before the NET Act was passed, a person could be punished for copyright infringement only if he or she made money.

This loophole first became an issue during a criminal trial against a Massachusetts Institute of Technology (MIT) student named David LaMacchia. LaMacchia transferred, or moved, computer games from one BBS to another BBS. Users of the

It can be easy and fun to find games, music, and movies on the Internet. But downloading copyrighted material without paying for it is illegal.

second BBS then could download them.[10] LaMacchia was found not guilty because he was not paid for the games.

Now, under the NET Act, anyone who reproduces or distributes copyrighted material electronically, regardless of his or her reason, can be prosecuted.[11] In other words, uploading a copy of a software program onto the Internet so that your friends can download it for free may now be a crime.

The Digital Millennium Copyright Act. President Bill Clinton signed the DMCA into law in October 1998.[12] Online copyright violations were uncertain under the Copyright Act of 1976. Congress enacted the DMCA to reduce this uncertainty. The DMCA also implemented the treaties signed in December 1996 at the World Intellectual Property Organization (WIPO) conference in Geneva.

Five parts of the DMCA address a number of issues. In general, the DMCA makes it a crime to circumvent or break the copy protection measures built into most commercial software.

The DMCA also outlaws the manufacture, sale, or distribution of code-cracking devices used to illegally copy software. However, it does permit the cracking of copyright protection devices to do encryption research. Encryption research is the legal study of the method or programming used to protect material. The DMCA also permits cracking copyright protection devices for authorized tests of computer security systems.

World Intellectual Property Organization. The WIPO is an international organization designed to protect intellectual property. Intellectual property is any product that has been created by someone and that has value. A computer program is an example of intellectual property.

WIPO is one of the specialized agencies within the United Nations. It has 177 member nations.[13] The organization upholds a number of international treaties, including the Berne Convention and the WIPO Copyright Treaty.

The Berne Convention for Protection of Literary and Artistic Works. This agreement was created in 1886 to recognize copyrights between countries.[14] Before the Berne Convention, nations sometimes refused to recognize the works of foreign nationals as copyrighted.[15] For example, if someone from the United Kingdom wrote an article, it would be protected by copyright in that country, but it could be reproduced freely in France, and vice versa. Under the Berne Convention that was no longer the case.

For the first hundred years after the Berne Convention was established, the United States refused to become a member of the convention because it would have required major changes in its copyright law. However, in 1988 the United States made the necessary changes and became part of the convention.

Copyright protection under the Berne Convention is automatic—the work does not have to be registered. The convention provides a minimum term of copyright protection—the life of the author plus fifty years.[16]

WIPO Copyright Treaty. This treaty was adopted by WIPO in 1996. It provides additional protections for copyright owners. Under the treaty, computer programs are protected as literary works. The arrangement and selection of material in databases also is protected.

Furthermore, the treaty gives the creators control over the rental and distribution of their work, and it prevents the circumvention of protection devices. In the United States, the WIPO Copyright Treaty is implemented through the DMCA.

Trade-Related Aspects of Intellectual Property Rights. Nicknamed the TRIPS Agreement, this is an international agreement regarding intellectual property. It covers everything from copyrights and patents to trademarks and trade secrets. Every member of the World Trade Organization (WTO) must enact the intellectual property laws of TRIPS in order to become a member of WTO.

Under TRIPS, computer programs are viewed as literary works through copyright law and receive the same terms of protection. Copyright terms must extend to fifty years after the death of the author, and copyright must be granted automatically.[17]

Today's File-Sharing Argument

Some people call it trading. Some people call it stealing. But whatever your views, there is a major argument raging today over peer-to-peer file sharing.

Since Napster burst onto the scene in 1999, file-swapping has grown from a favorite pastime among college students to an international phenomenon.[18] Consequently, millions of copies of digital media are exchanged every day. According to Websense Inc., a provider of employee Internet management software, peer-to-peer networks are now trading more than MP3s, including anything from the latest episode of *The Sopranos* to popular video games.

As a result, the variety of files available is encouraging the creation of new p2p Web sites and applications. The number of peer-to-peer file-sharing Web pages has increased more than 300 percent, totaling more than 89,000 Web pages.[19] There are more than 130 unique peer-to-peer applications, such as Kazaa and Grokster.

"P2P networks have truly developed beyond the music to become a marketplace for users swapping videos, games and software packages," says Harold Kester, chief technology officer for Websense Inc.[20]

Although trading MP3s remains popular, trading of other content is also increasing. In some cases, other uses are on par with music swapping. For example, more than 5 billion music files were downloaded from p2p networks last year, according to a research firm, The Yankee Group. More than 5 million video game downloads also occurred last year, according to game developer Trymedia, and between 400,000 and 600,000 copies of movies are downloaded each day, according to a consulting firm, Viant. About 3 million users download favorite TV shows, such as *Buffy the Vampire Slayer*, from Kazaa every day.[21] All of this downloading has created an intense argument over copyrights.

On one side of the debate, you have the argument for freedom of speech, right to privacy, fair use, and the importance of encouraging technological advances. On the other side, you have the argument for copyright protection, ownership of intellectual property, and the right to be paid for creating various works.

While both sides of the debate present good arguments, to date the law has sided mostly with copyright owners. For many, this debate is far from being settled. For every legal victory and technological advance the copyright industries make, those who want to share copyrighted material freely always seem to stay one step ahead.[22]

Free Speech? The Argument for the Underground Internet

Technology is at the center of many people's argument for peer-to-peer file sharing. To many, sharing digital media, whether it is music, movies, or software, is nothing more than a technological advance. It is a way to make our lives simpler and more efficient. Many feel this advance should be accepted by everyone, including the copyright industries. After all, they argue, this country prides itself on the technological advances it makes each year.

Supporters of file sharing say the original purpose of the Internet was to be a peer-to-peer system. They maintain that the current crop of peer-to-peer applications use the Internet for the purpose it was originally designed—as a way for machines to communicate with each other and share files and information.[1] Although there are a number of individuals and organizations that support p2p file sharing, the most notable and organized groups include the Electronic Frontier Foundation (EFF), the Digital Future Coalition, the Electronic Privacy Information Center, the Global Internet Liberty Campaign, and the Center for Democracy and Technology. For the most part, these groups fight for issues like free speech, right to privacy, and minimal government regulation.

When it comes to p2p file sharing, these groups believe that the movie and recording studios are trying to "dumb down" (or simplify) technology. They accuse them of using copyright laws to benefit intellectual property ownership while hurting the consumer's right to freedom.

Supporters of file sharing also believe the Digital Millennium Copyright Act (DMCA) passed in 1998 has caused some unintended consequences. The DMCA is often used to prove copyright infringement. Among the top concerns is that the DMCA hurts free expression and scientific research, puts fair use at risk, and interferes with competition and innovation.[2]

What Is "Fair Use"?

Under United States copyright law, copyright holders have the exclusive right to reproduce works for a limited time period. "Fair use" is a limitation of this right. Basically, it allows the public to use copyrighted work without having to ask permission, as long the use does not interfere with the copyright owner's market for the work.

Fair use can include personal, noncommercial uses, such as using a VCR to record a television program to watch later. It also can include using the material for activities such as teaching, research, reviewing, and news reporting.

Supporters of file sharing claim that innovations in the way music is distributed can offer artists new opportunities.

Supporters of file sharing accuse the copyright industries of overstating the threat of Internet piracy to keep artists dependent on them. They claim the entertainment industry has made money from artists for years by offering to reproduce and distribute their songs in exchange for the artists' copyrights. According to the EFF, however, "new technologies are dramatically reducing artists' dependence on these traditional industry services, taking away a large bargaining chip corporations had with artists."[3] As a result, they believe the industry has attacked the tools that can give artists their independence. What's more, supporters fear that the copyright industries will cause significant damage to developers of this new technology in their zeal to stop illegal trading.

Does Downloading Really Affect Music Sales?

Piracy did not cause the 15 percent drop in music sales in the past two years, according to an August 2002 report from Forrester Research, a Massachusetts-based technology research company.[4]

The company says record labels can help the industry grow again by making it easier for consumers to find, copy, and pay for music on their own terms. Tyler, a 25-year-old software developer, agrees. "Normally, albums have a few great tunes, a few good tunes and the rest, well, they sort of [stink]," he says. "[It would be nice] to just download my favorite tunes and burn my own CDs."[5]

"There is no denying that times are tough for the music business, but not because of downloading," says Josh Bernoff, principal analyst at Forrester. "Based on surveys of 1,000 online consumers we see no evidence of decreased CD buying among frequent digital music consumers. Plenty of other causes are [possible], including the economic recession and competition from [growing] video game and DVD sales."[6]

The report also indicates that:

- Consumers want to find music from any label, not just two or three.
- Consumers want the right to control their music by burning it onto CDs or copying it onto an MP3 player.[7]

Forrester predicts that by 2005 downloading will start to soar, and by 2007 digital music revenues will make up 17 percent of the music business. Furthermore, the company predicts that by 2007, digital music revenues will reach more than $2 billion. (Revenue is the total income produced by a single source.) As a result, Forrester says, artists will embrace the Internet and sign downloading rights over to their labels.[8]

Peer-to-Peer Technology, Copyrights, and Piracy

The majority of peer-to-peer technology supporters understand the need to protect copyrights. They also recognize the need to reduce piracy of digital content.

According to the Center for Democracy and Technology, the growing use of peer-to-peer networks has created a lot of new problems for copyright holders. Peer-to-peer can be a great tool for users. Even so, its use by copyright infringers can pose a great threat to creators and distributors of music, movies, video games, books, and software.[9]

At the same time, p2p supporters worry that consumers' rights will be trampled in the regulation process—specifically, their rights to free expression, fair use, and privacy. Furthermore, they are concerned that too many controls will destroy the promise that p2p technology holds for the future of the Internet. In general, they do not support any laws or technological steps that will hurt legal uses of the technology.

"Solutions that provide the [copyright] industry with a reasonably secure digital environment for its content can coexist with citizens' rights under copyright law," says Gigi Sohn, president of Public Knowledge, an advocacy group. She says these solutions can also provide "continued access to an open Internet and the kind of flexible technology that [citizens] have come to expect and enjoy."[10]

Overall, p2p supporters present three main arguments against too much regulation and too many controls. These arguments include:

- free expression and scientific research
- "fair use" and right to privacy
- innovation and competition

The Free-Expression and Scientific-Research Arguments

The right to speak freely is one of our country's most prized freedoms. It is a freedom that supporters of peer-to-peer technology fear will be trampled on in an effort to enforce copyrights.

"It's very clear that reckless copyright enforcement can [hurt free] speech," says Siva Valdhyanathan, author of *Copyrights and Copywrongs: The Rise of Intellectual Property and How It Threatens Creativity.* "Once you increase [copyright] protection to an absurd level, you end up having a negative effect."[11]

More specifically, peer-to-peer supporters believe that the DMCA is being used by a number of copyright owners to hold back free speech and scientific research. They cite numerous court battles to support their position.

For instance, in September 2000, Secure Digital Music Initiative (SDMI), a group of more than 160 companies and organizations, issued a public challenge. They encouraged technology experts to try to beat their watermarking technologies. These technologies were designed to protect digital music.

Princeton professor Edward Felten and a team of researchers from various other universities took up the challenge and succeeded in removing the watermarks. But when the team tried to present their results at an academic conference, the RIAA and SDMI threatened to take legal action. The RIAA and SDMI claimed that the DMCA makes it illegal to discuss or provide technology that might be used to bypass industry controls.

The professor, his research team, and their legal representatives from the EFF argued that they had a First Amendment right to present their research. Like most scientists, they wanted to discuss their findings. They also wanted to publish a paper describing the weaknesses of several technologies they had studied. They argued that openly discussing customer control technologies would result in improved technology and better consumer choice.[12]

"When scientists are intimidated from publishing their work, there is a clear First Amendment problem," says EFF legal director Cindy Cohn. "We have long argued that . . . the anti-distribution provisions of the DMCA would interfere with science. Now they plainly have."[13]

Supporters of p2p technology argue that online service providers and bulletin board operators are starting to censor discussions about how to overcome copy-protection systems. They also cite examples where students, scientists, and security experts have stopped publishing details of their research on security protocols. Furthermore, foreign scientists are uneasy about traveling to the United States for fear of possible DMCA liability.[14] As a result, some technical conferences have been relocated overseas.

Ultimately, some people believe, these developments will result in less security for all computer users, including copyright owners who are depending on technical methods to protect their works. Security researchers will avoid doing research that might make them a target for legal action under the DMCA.[15]

The Fair-Use and Right-to-Privacy Arguments

Halting copyright infringement is important, but many people fear that copyright owners will use technology to prevent piracy and ultimately take away fair use. They also worry that no future fair uses will be developed because copyright owners say that these tools also can result in piracy.

"The traditional answer for piracy under copyright law has been to seek out and prosecute the infringers, not to ban the tools that enable fair use," according to the EFF. "After all, photocopiers, videocassette recorders [VCRs], and CD-R [compact disc recorder] burners can also be misused, but no one would suggest that the public give them up simply because they might be used by others to break the law."[16]

Introducing items like copy-protected CDs is not the answer either, critics say. Even though copy-protected CDs may have an impact on online file sharing, many people believe they also are interfering with the consumer's right to fair use.

For instance, copy-protected CDs will disappoint the hundreds of thousands of consumers who have purchased MP3 players and want to make MP3 copies of their own CDs. Making an MP3 copy of a CD you own for personal use is an example of fair use. Other examples of fair use that could be harmed by copy-protection technologies are making "mix CDs" or copies of CDs for the office or car.

Moreover, companies that distribute tools to "repair" these CDs—in order to restore fair-use privileges—run the risk of lawsuits under the DMCA's ban on circumvention tools and technology.[17]

Copy-Protection Technologies and Privacy

Many people fear that the consumer's right to privacy is also being threatened by copy-protection technology. This technology is often called digital rights management (DRM). DRM is designed to provide more security for copyrighted materials. These technologies can control how many times you are allowed to look at something, and how long you can view it. Your ability to change the material, share it, copy it, print it, and save it can be limited.

Critics argue that copyright holders are abusing this technology. Some DRM technologies have been developed with little regard for privacy protection. For example, many systems require the users to identify themselves and their rights to the content in order to view the material. By doing so, a person's right to view something anonymously has been taken away.

Some DRM technologies may harm a user's PC. For instance, a Celine Dion album released in 2002 by EPIC records and Sony records can crash a user's computer if the disc is inserted into a CD-ROM drive. Critics argue that many of these copy-protected CDs are not properly labeled.[18]

Finally, DRM is being used to monitor how people use material. As a result, profiles of each user's preferences are created. For example, Microsoft Windows Media Player creates a log file of the content a user views and "phones home" to a central server with a list of content titles.[19] Media Player allows people to watch downloaded or streamed video. For example, CNBC streams their newscasts and programs (or shows them live) over the Internet. If someone uses Media Player to watch CNBC or some other program, the company has the ability to track what that person is watching. Knowledge like that is an invasion of privacy and can lead to unfair practices like price discrimination, says the Electronic Privacy Information Center (EPIC). (Price discrimination is setting a price based on knowledge of the consumer's desire for something.) In other words, the price would be set higher because the company knows the person wants the product or service and would be willing to pay more for it.[20]

According to EPIC, these technologies mark an important development in the use of copyright law. Now copyright is being used as a justification to both protect content and profile the consumers of content, they say.[21]

The Innovation and Competition Argument

Many organizations claim that copyright owners are concentrating on their competitors rather than focusing on pirates—and that they are using the DMCA to do so. Specifically, they claim that copyright holders are using the act's anticircumvention provision against scientists, competitors, and consumers and not against pirates as was originally intended. (The anticircumvention provision of the DMCA makes it a crime to break copy-protection systems except for authorized research and testing.)

To support their claim, critics use a number of court cases as examples. One example involves Lexmark, a printer company. In 2002, Lexmark sued Static Control Components (SCC). They accused SCC of developing "Smartek" chips. These chips allow cheaper toner cartridges to work in Lexmark printers. (Before, only Lexmark's toner cartridges would work in their printers.) To create the chips, SCC reverse engineered, or took apart, Lexmark's authentication routines. These were mechanisms designed to prevent other companies from creating toner cartridges that would work in Lexmark's printers. Lexmark argued under the DMCA that SCC had circumvented

Many people fear that the consumer's right to privacy is being threatened by copy-protection technology. For example, many systems require users to identify themselves and their rights to the content in order to view the material. By doing so, a person's right to view something anonymously has been taken away.

their program. Critics respond that it is simply innovation.

"Whatever the merits of Lexmark's position, it is fair to say that eliminating the laser printer toner aftermarket was not what Congress had in mind when enacting the DMCA," the EFF says.[22]

Another example is the way in which Sony has used the DMCA to pressure its competitors. Sony has sued companies that created software that allowed PC owners to play games made for the Sony Playstation, a video game console.

Sony sued both Connectix Corporation and Bleem. Connectix created the Virtual Game Station, which allowed Sony Playstation games to be played on Apple computers. Bleem was the top seller of software for Windows PCs.

The two companies argued that they had created their products through reverse engineering. Reverse engineering has been interpreted as fair use in several court cases, including a case in which the Ninth Circuit Court .3in California found in favor of Connectix.[23] However, the two companies could not afford to fight a legal battle with Sony and were forced to pull their products off the market.

The Digital Media Consumers' Rights Act

Representative Rick Boucher of Virginia introduced the Digital Media Consumers' Rights Act to Congress. Under the act, it would not be a violation of the DMCA to circumvent a technological measure as long as it is not copyright infringement. The act also requires proper labeling of copy-protected CDs and changes the DMCA so that scientists can create software tools to research copy-protection systems.[24]

"The bill seeks to restore the balance in our nation's copyright laws in ways that will promote technological innovation and consumer freedom," says Boucher, "while at the same time ensuring that record companies, movie studios and book producers can stop pirates from stealing."[25]

Other Arguments

While free speech, fair use, privacy, and research are among the top reasons people support peer-to-peer technology, there are several other arguments that people make with regard to peer-to-peer. These include comparing p2p with the introduction of the VCR and describing what a powerful tool peer-to-peer can be for unsigned artists. (Artists who are unsigned are not under contract with a record company.)

"P2P is no more threatening than the VCR." Downloaders say that copyright owners are notorious for crying "foul" when it comes to new technology. They think that copyright owners are overreacting because they do not fully understand new technologies like p2p and assume it is threatening to them.

One example of this overreaction, they say, is the famous Sony Betamax case, which involved the creation of the VCR. In 1984, the U.S. Supreme Court said that Sony was not liable for copyright infringement just because buyers of the Betamax VCR used it to record copyrighted television programs to watch later.

The Supreme Court said this type of "time shifting" was allowed because the television networks meant for people to see the shows. All the Betamax did was allow them to watch the show at a different time. Additionally, the Supreme Court said that Sony had lost contact with the purchaser after the sale and had no way of knowing about infringements by the user later. The copyright industry lost the legal battle, and the public now enjoys the VCR. The interesting fact is that the very thing the industry was fighting—the VCR—is now a very big part of their business. The movie industry makes a lot of money from video rentals and video sales each year.

Other examples of overreaction include industry fears about recording albums onto cassette tapes and the use of copy machines to make copies of copyrighted work. In both instances, the copyright industries were not hurt by these new technologies. If anything, critics say, they benefited from them. They argue that the same thing can happen to the industry if peer-to-peer is allowed to reach its potential.

Megan, a 22-year-old college graduate, believes that musicians and record labels who have become upset over file sharing have a weak argument:

> Libraries lend books to customers without any money exchanged but I haven't heard authors or publishing companies complaining about the loss of money in book sales because of it. Instead, one might even argue that MP3 sharing actually gives the artist more exposure and gets the media in the hands of more people and more potential fans.[26]

P2P supporters caution that in many respects, it is a little too late now—that the RIAA should have embraced the technology sooner and tried to work with Napster rather than shutting it down. After all, Napster already had consumer loyalty and a very big share of the market.

Instead, when the RIAA successfully shut Napster down with legal action, they paved the way for other file-sharing services to pick up the slack. As a result, this new brand of services is much harder to fight, because, unlike Napster, they do not have a central server or one person to go after. So, in essence, the RIAA has made things more difficult for itself.

What's more, now that the RIAA has embraced the technology as something that can be used to copyright owners' benefit, it faces an uphill battle in getting downloaders to support it.

"P2P is a way for musicians to get noticed." Many musicians—especially independent and unknown artists—see the Internet as an excellent promotional tool. Using MP3 technology and peer-to-peer networks, unsigned artists can reach a huge audience, and build a base of fans with the hope of getting noticed.

Music fans like Megan insist that people would still purchase CDs of their favorite artists, even if they have already downloaded the songs. "A true fan would also still pay to see their favorite band or musician in concert," she says. "Nothing online will ever replace live performances." Megan, who enjoys music by everyone from Norah Jones and Guster to Jason Mraz and Phantom Planet, says she has seen nine of her favorite bands in concert, four of them more than once.

"I also have purchased each of their CDs, even though I had access to free online files," she adds. "True fans will pay for the real deal even when free versions are available."[27]

Supporters of file sharing believe that the Internet has been a big help to independent record labels, entrepreneurs, songwriters, and artists. It has given artists a new way to gain exposure without a contract from a major record label.

For example, musicians are gaining exposure through file-sharing Web sites like Garageband.com. Since 1999, Garageband says that thirteen bands have been signed by major record labels. One has already gone double platinum. They claim that many more bands have scored publishing, production, or licensing deals, which in some cases was because of exposure on Garageband.[28]

One argument for file sharing is that it offers new artists a way to get noticed without having to sign with a recording company.

One band discovered through Garageband is Roman Candle, which signed a contract with Hollywood Records. Originally, the band was signed by Trevor Pryce of the independent label Outlook Music. Pryce discovered them on Garageband's Track of the Day. This success eventually led to two songs being featured on MTV's *Real World vs. Road Rules.* The songs were "Something Left to Say" and "You Don't Belong to This World." The band was featured in *Rolling Stone* and *Gear Magazine,* and they secured gigs with the Wallflowers, Patti Smith, and Edwin McCain.

According to band member Logan Matheny,

> When we first put our songs up on Garageband.com, we loved getting reviews from Amsterdam and Australia. But once Trevor Pryce e-mailed us after downloading our music and wanted to sign us, we knew more than just bands trying to make it were paying attention to this site. If it weren't for this site, we would still be working first shift in the warehouse. Garageband is an amazing way to make a fan base before you even have an album out! We still hear from people who first heard our music on this site.[29]

MP3 technology and peer-to-peer file sharing can return the power of song ownership to the artists. For some artists, the ability to reach a larger audience without touring or being tied to a recording contract may seem a dream come true. Currently, when an artist signs a deal with a record label, they sign over the rights to their music to the label. In exchange, the label pays for everything needed up front to record the music, market it, and sell it. In a sense, the record label is the middleman between artists and their fans. Most of the profits from music sales then go to the record label to help cover their initial costs and the risks they took in signing the artist. The artist gets a small percentage of the sales income, but they no longer "own" the music. The record label owns it.

Supporters of p2p technology maintain that the Internet makes it possible to reduce the cost of packaging and distributing music, which is where record companies currently spend most of the money that could be going to artists. In addition, they believe that by using the Internet and p2p technology, tools can be developed that empower artists to take control of their own art and to be compensated appropriately for their works.

Finally, the decision of what sells and what is listened to would no longer be determined by who the record labels want to promote, supporters say. The choice would be returned to the consumer.

Currently, record stores usually carry only about 6 percent of all available CDs. Consumers can listen only to the artists that the labels decide to promote. That's why the MP3 movement started on university campuses, where students short on cash are looking for the next new sound and rising artists.[30]

One thing is for sure—consumers want to get their music online. Not only is it more convenient and flexible but it also offers a better selection. Megan says,

> I think swapping music online is wonderful. It [allows people] to hear many different artists and types of music that [they] otherwise would never have experienced. I think it encourages people to find new and different stuff besides the same old, same old that we hear on the radio everyday. [Online file sharing] puts the control of what we listen to into the hands of the listeners. . . . The decision of what we hear is no longer up to just the radio stations and the record labels.[31]

Copyright Infringement? The Argument Against the Underground Internet

Copyright is at the heart of the copyright industry's fight against online file sharing. Anyone who has ever created something—a song, movie, software package, painting, or book—knows that some protection against copying their work is essential to survival. After all, piracy of copyrighted material chips away at the creator's livelihood.

Many people do not understand the significant harm caused by piracy. Both the entertainment industry and the software industry still seem to be making money, and the artists and creators are still getting rich. The general thinking is, "Downloading a few songs, an occasional movie, or a software program isn't going to hurt anyone."

But that's simply not the case. For example, 85 percent of music recordings do not generate enough money to cover their costs. Record companies depend on the remaining 15 percent of recordings to pay for the less profitable types of music, to cover costs of developing new artists, and to keep their businesses running. Because of piracy, musicians, singers, songwriters, and producers do not get the royalties and fees they have earned.[1]

The same is true for the movie and software industries. Moviemaking is very risky. According to the Motion Picture Association of America, only one out of ten films ever recovers its investment from domestic exhibition. Four out of ten movies never get back the original investment at all. In 2000, the average major studio film cost $55 million to produce and an extra $27 million to advertise and market.[2]

Software developers also suffer greatly from piracy. Money lost from software piracy reaches billions of dollars every year. Developers count on the money made from software package sales to recover costs invested in developing the software. They also use the money to pay for research and development for future software programs. If there is not enough money to support research and development, then the developers cannot pay their employees or hire new ones. In 2000, it is estimated that 118,000 people lost their jobs and $5.7 billion in wages were lost due to software piracy in the United States alone.[3]

Overall, the copyright industry's argument is pretty simple. First, copyright holders deserve to be protected not only because it is the law, but also because they are investing their time, money, and hard work to create something. They have a right to be paid for their work. Piracy takes that right away. By not enforcing copyrights, we also run the risk that creative work will eventually vanish because there is no incentive or money to produce anything.

Secondly, piracy of copyrighted material is stealing and should not be tolerated any more than shoplifting is tolerated.

If hundreds of thousands of movies were stolen from video stores instead of Web sites, no one would be defending the shoplifters with claims of personal freedom.[4]

Finally, they argue that they need to be able to protect their creations by using copy-protection technology known as digital rights management (DRM), lawsuits against infringers, and legislation.

The Copyright Industries' View of the Internet and P2P Technology

The following figures show the size of the Internet piracy problem:

- An estimated 3.6 billion songs or files are being copied per month.
- About 350,000 to 400,000 films are downloaded each day through file-sharing programs.
- Reducing software piracy to lower levels could produce a million additional jobs and nearly $25 billion in additional government revenues worldwide by 2005.[5]

The growth of the Internet in the last ten years has demonstrated its enormous potential. It also has improved our lives in a number of ways. The Internet allows us to communicate without geographic boundaries; it provides us with the ability to send and receive information quickly; and it gives us access to all types of information.

As a whole, the copyright industries understand this fact. Contrary to popular belief, they are not anti-Internet. They recognize, like everyone else, that the Internet has the potential to be a great way to deliver material to an enormous audience.[6]

Copyright industries are not antitechnology. They have not only embraced new technologies, but they also have thrived on them. For example, the pioneering of special effects by moviemakers has revitalized computer graphic and audiovisual technologies.[7]

The record industry has never really had a problem with file sharing—just with widespread file sharing. CD burning and file swapping between friends is not generally viewed as a problem. Some labels worry about upsetting their customers who want to share files and burn CDs. Record companies in general do not want to interfere with somebody who makes a mix CD. The problem is not with personal use, but with widespread sharing on a huge scale.[8]

They also know that if used inappropriately, the Internet and peer-to-peer technology pose a very real threat to both the copyright industries and intellectual property. Perhaps one of the biggest threats comes in the form of illegal copying, or piracy. Piracy reduces a creator's desire to invest in developing something—whether it is a song, a movie, a software program, or a book. Piracy also has an impact on the widespread availability of legitimate intellectual property online. For the Internet to reach its full potential—as a source of education, entertainment, and productivity—high-value copyrighted works must be protected online.[9]

P2P: Use vs. Abuse

Peer-to-peer technology is an exciting technology that has a number of legitimate uses. The problem—argue the copyright industries—is how this technology is being used, or rather abused, today.

There are a number of peer-to-peer network protocols available. Two of the most popular are the FastTrack and the Gnutella networks, both of which have been extremely successful. There are about 4.5 million users on the FastTrack Network at any given moment, and those users are distributing more than 880 million different files. Kazaa (using the FastTrack network) and Morpheus (using the Gnutella network) are collecting more than $450,000 per month from advertising alone.[10]

According to Matthew J. Oppenheim of the RIAA,

For the copyright industry, the problem has not been so much with people who make copies for their own use, but with sharing on a huge scale.

All of this success should come as no surprise. These companies are building businesses off of the backs of others. They pay nothing to the creators . . . of the music that is driving their business. They invest nothing in the marketing and promotion of the music, and they take no risks in supporting new and developing artists. Without leeching from others, p2p businesses could not exist.[11]

The sole purpose of these networks, the industry says, is copyright infringement. Evidence shows that 90 percent of the works distributed on the FastTrack network and 99 percent of the audio files requested on the Gnutella network are copyrighted.[12]

Even worse, this technology is being used for a number of less-than-desirable purposes. First, users can unknowingly share information and files they never intended to. For example, you could share a copy of your financial records or private letters and e-mails without even knowing it. Secondly, some file-sharing services install spyware—a program that secretly collects information on what the users are doing on their PCs. Finally, users (including young children) can access or be exposed to pornography.

File Sharing and Pornography

As a whole, file-sharing programs are seen as a way to get free music, movies, and software online, but there is a darker side. These programs also are widely used as a way to access pornography. (Pornography is inappropriate sexually explicit material.)

The pornographic material is free, and it is not usually blocked by parental control software or filters. (These are software programs installed on computers to limit the types of material that can be accessed.) What this means is that some children are able to view pornography without their parents' knowledge.

Even if young people are using these programs for other purposes, such as getting copies of favorite songs and movies, they still can be exposed to pornography. For instance, if one searches for popular names like Britney Spears, Christina Aguilera, or Madonna on a popular file-sharing service, more than 70 percent of the results are pornographic files.[13]

Overall, this trend to use peer-to-peer file sharing to access sexually explicit material has alarmed a lot of people. In addition to graphic adult videos, the content includes child pornography and violent pornography. According to a U.S. House of Representatives report, searches for "preteen," "rape," and "incest," are among the top searches or requests made each day through some p2p file-sharing services.[14]

Protecting Copyrights in the Digital Age

The Internet has created huge opportunities for all types of businesses, including the copyright industries. Unlike traditional distribution channels, it is relatively easy and inexpensive to set up Web sites to get material out there. And because of the vast size and reach of the Internet, businesses can reach millions of people almost instantly.

By the same token, these characteristics can be a real disadvantage as well—especially when material can be copied so easily and distributed without permission. Currently, online piracy poses the biggest threat to copyright protection. As a result, it has become increasingly important to protect copyrights.

On the one hand, online file sharing does not appear any worse than dubbing a cassette tape, says Allison, an employee of an Internet marketing agency.

> We've all done it [dubbed a cassette tape] at one time or another, and there typically are no repercussions. But as somebody who works for a living in a "creative" field, where the value of your work is less tangible, I can understand [the need to protect copyrights and profit from your work].[15]

There is no one answer to fighting piracy in the Digital Age. Instead, the copyright industries have come to realize that to effectively fight piracy they need to do a variety of things. First, it is obvious that customers like the convenience and speed of getting music, movies, and software online. As a result, the industry is developing some creative ways to meet the customer's desire and still make money. They are making great strides in this area.

Secondly, they need to take steps that will enable them to protect their copyrights. Some of this protection can be accomplished using copy-protection technology or digital rights management.

Finally, they need to continue to bring lawsuits against infringers and work with lawmakers to improve copyright laws. By doing so, they can meet the challenges posed by anonymous file-sharing programs that are used for illegal purposes.

Why Protect the Copyright Industries?

An economic study, *Copyright Industries in the U.S. Economy: The 2001 Report*, released in 2002, indicated that the copyright-based industries such as the music, movie, and publishing industries are the United States' largest and fastest growing economic assets. These creative industries contributed more to the U.S. economy, and employed more workers, than any single manufacturing sector.[16]

Consequently, many people argue that in order to promote a thriving economy in the United States we need to protect its most valuable contributors—the copyright industries.

Following is an overview of the ways in which the copyright industry impacts the U.S. economy:

- In 2001, the U.S. copyright industries accounted for an estimated 5.24 percent of the U.S. gross domestic product (GDP), or $535.1 billion.

- Between 1977 and 2001, employment in the U.S. copyright industries more than doubled to 4.7 million workers.

- Over the last twenty-four years (1977–2001) the U.S. copyright industries' share of GDP grew more than twice as fast as the remainder of the economy (7 percent versus 3 percent annually).[17]

The Copyright Protection Argument

Today's copyright laws are the result of technological changes, including everything from Gutenberg's movable type to VCRs to digital audio recorders. Since its inception, copyright law has changed and responded to technological changes. It is apparent

**Artists and other copyright holders want to protect their work from piracy.
Shown is musician John Mayer in Las Vegas in 2004.**

that technology continues to have an enormous impact on the ways in which copyrighted material is created, reproduced, and distributed.

Digital technology in particular is challenging the ability of copyright owners to authorize or prohibit the use of their material. This problem is seen in the large amount of file sharing that takes place every day. This file trading of copyrighted material, without the copyright owner's permission, is against the law. This is why the RIAA won its case against Napster.

Although people may debate the details of the law, to date the courts have held that sharing copies of copyrighted music, movies, and software without permission through peer-to-peer systems is illegal. Simply put, it is piracy—a huge worldwide problem that robs creators while driving up costs for consumers.

Creating songs, movies, books, and software is hard work. It also is time-consuming and expensive. Yet the finished products can be stolen in a matter of seconds online, and the creators lose money in the process.

Aside from the sheer pleasure of the work, it is the pay-off in the end that inspires many creators to invest their time and money to create something. It is the assurance of copyright protection that gives them peace of mind that they will not only be protected, but also be paid for their hard work.

For companies and individuals to continue moving their work into the digital world, they need to know that their creations will not be ripped off by pirates who can copy them and send them around the world with the click of a mouse.

Just because technology makes it easy to copy and distribute creative works digitally does not mean that any individual or enterprise has the absolute right to copy, steal, or otherwise trample on intellectual property laws in the name of fair use.[18]

The Copy-Protection Systems Argument

Digital media, such as music, films, and books can be copied, distributed, and consumed in a matter of minutes, thanks to the Internet. Consequently, downloading files has become increasingly popular because it provides immediate access to the material and does not require a trip to the mall.

The obvious answer would appear to be, "Put your material online." However, the copyright industries have been slow to make their products available for sale online, because they are concerned about protecting their work from piracy.

One way to ensure protection of their material is through copy-protection technology, known as digital rights management technology, or DRM. In most cases, DRM is a system that encrypts digital media content. If something is encrypted, it has been changed into a format that is not easily understood by unauthorized people.

DRM also can limit access to only those people who have a license to play or use the content. Overall, DRM is a way by which copyright holders can promote, sell, and distribute digital media on the Internet. Supporters argue that it gives copyright holders the security they need to distribute material online while providing consumers with the online convenience they want.

Other businesses also are looking into DRM's potential, including law firms, financial companies, and publishers. One reason for this increased interest is theft. In a 2002 survey by PricewaterhouseCoopers and the U.S. Chamber of Commerce, 138 companies said they lost between $53 billion and $59 billion in 2001 from theft of their intellectual property and other information, including research, customer lists, and financial data. Such thefts resulted in increased legal fees, loss of money, and loss of competitive advantage.[19]

Two Types of Protective Technology

Encryption Envelope: This encrypted software creates a "secure container" around the material that keeps the content away from other people while in the user's hands and prevents the material from being changed.

Digital Watermarking: This software allows copyright owners to insert a digital stamp into their data that acts as a copyright statement and travels with the material throughout its use.

The Improved-Legislation Argument

Currently, most peer-to-peer networks are being used for piracy. Downloads from these systems consist mainly of

---

DRM at Its Best

Following is an example of how the British rock band Oasis used DRM to protect its copyrights while publicizing its new CD.

The Situation: Oasis wanted to create a buzz for the release of its 2002 CD, *Heathen Chemistry*, by promoting certain songs before the CD hit the store shelves.

The Problem: The band's record company, Big Brother Recordings Ltd., which is part of Sony Music Entertainment Inc., knew that giving fans advance copies of the music could kill any chances of making money. They had no doubt that the songs would end up being shared online through p2p networks.

The Solution: On June 23, 2002, nearly 2 million Britons opened their London *Sunday Times* paper to find a free CD containing three not-yet-released song clips from the band's new album. Using DRM, Sony had encoded the CDs to keep people from playing the clips more than just a few times on their PCs. Fans also were unable to copy the music and post it on file-sharing programs. Oasis fans could link to the band's Web site to preorder the new album or wait until it was released.

The Results: Preorders of the album exceeded company expectations by 30,000 during the week following the *Sunday Times* promotion, and the number of visitors to the band's Web site increased.[20]

DRM technology helps copyright holders control how their creations are used. One type of CD will crash a user's computer if inserted into the CD-ROM drive.

copyrighted music, movies, and software. And as the systems are perfected and downloading speeds improve, the amount of copyrighted material that is stolen each day will increase as well.

For the most part, the owners and creators of the copyrighted material have not authorized the use or distribution of their material through these file-sharing programs. Distribution of this size and magnitude in no way fits the definition of fair use. As a result, there is no question that the vast majority of downloading is copyright infringement and that copyright owners and creators are being robbed daily.

To combat this problem, the copyright industries are lobbying to improve copyright laws. One piece of legislation that would allow copyright holders to confront peer-to-peer piracy head-on is the Piracy Deterrence and Education Act (HR2517). If passed, this legislation would give copyright owners the right to use a variety of technological tools to prevent illegal copying and distribution of their material.

6 Underground Internet Lawsuits and Their Outcomes

The creation of peer-to-peer file-sharing programs has been wonderful for downloaders of free music, movies, and software, but it also has turned copyright law on its head. According to an article in *The Economist*, the "copyright battle is becoming one of the most urgent and bitterly fought because it could yet determine the future character of cyberspace itself."[1]

Perhaps the most noteworthy legal battle was the one between the RIAA and Napster. With the Napster case, the software maker was held liable for the illegal activities of people using their software. In a widely used peer-to-peer file-sharing setting like Napster, the court said that it should be expected that at least some of the users would participate in illegal activities. As a result, Napster was eventually shut down because of copyright infringement.

Timeline of the Napster Case

May 1999: Napster began to gain popularity, primarily on college campuses, where students have easy access to high-speed Internet connections.

December 1999: The RIAA sued Napster in the U.S. district court in San Francisco on grounds of copyright infringement.

May 2000: In federal court in San Francisco, Judge Marilyn Patel ruled that Napster was in violation of the Digital Millennium Copyright Act of 1998.

July 2000: Judge Patel ordered Napster to shut down. Patel said that Napster users were not simply engaging in swapping their personal favorite songs, and the song-swapping service was encouraging "wholesale infringing" against the music industry. Napster said they would appeal the decision.

February 2001: The Ninth Circuit Court of Appeals ruled that Napster users were illegally copying and distributing copyrighted commercial songs. It ordered Napster to stop its users from trading and distributing copyrighted material. However, the ruling allowed Napster to continue operating until Judge Patel's injunction was modified to comply with the appeal court's decision.

March 2001: Judge Patel issued an injunction, telling record companies to provide Napster with the exact file names of the copyrighted material. The RIAA provided Napster with a list from the five major record labels of approximately 135,000 copyrighted songs that the labels wanted removed from the song-swapping service. The RIAA filed a brief claiming that Napster had not complied with the injunction requiring removal of copyrighted material from its service.

June 2001: The Ninth Circuit Court of Appeals upheld its ruling that Napster had contributed to copyright infringement.

July 2001: Napster was ordered offline until it proved it was 100 percent free of copyrighted work.

March 2002: Napster was ordered to remain offline by a federal appeals court.

June 2002: Napster filed for Chapter 11 bankruptcy.[2]

November 2002: Following bankruptcy, Napster sold its patents and brand name to CD-burning software firm Roxio, pending court approval.[3]

December 2002: A Delaware bankruptcy court approved the sale of Napster to Roxio.[4]

February 2003: Roxio announced plans to relaunch Napster as a label-licensed, for-pay subscription service in late 2003. Shawn Fanning was hired as a consultant.[5]

October 2003: Roxio launched Napster 2.0 with industry support.

Some people thought that after Napster was gone, digital piracy also would be gone; others believed it was just the beginning. Recent lawsuits show, though, that the war against online piracy is still in full swing.

Instead of putting an end to file sharing of copyrighted material with the Napster lawsuit, more and more companies have popped up. The result has been some interesting lawsuits.

Notable Lawsuits and Criminal Cases

The Recording Industry Association of America has led the way when it comes to lawsuits against online pirates, beginning with the notorious legal battle with Napster. Since then, the RIAA has filed suits against other file-sharing services, including Kazaa, Morpheus, and Grokster. The organization has subpoenaed an Internet service provider (ISP) for the name of a subscriber and has sued college students for pirating music.

Following the legal action against Napster, the company reopened in 2003 as a legal service where songs could be downloaded for a fee. Here the rapper Ludacris looks at his songs online.

The Motion Picture Association of America (MPAA) and the software industry also have been active in filing lawsuits against infringers. Among the most notable are the cases against a Norwegian teenager and a Russian programmer.

The groups have also warned the heads of the nation's thousand biggest companies that corporations could be liable for violating copyright laws if employees use company networks to download, store, or distribute music or movies illegally. One early RIAA lawsuit—against an Arizona-based company, for storing illegal MP3s on the company's servers—was settled out of court for $1 million.[6]

Listed below is an overview of several cases and their outcomes.

Motion Picture Industry DeCSS Case. On August 17, 2000, a judge ruled in favor of the Motion Picture Association of America (MPAA). The decision barred Eric Corley and his *2600 Magazine* from posting DeCSS on his Web site and from linking to other Web sites where it was posted.[7] DeCSS is software that copies an encrypted DVD file and saves the file on a hard disk, allegedly minus the encryption. DeCSS also allows people to fast-forward through commercials and to make copies. In this case, DeCSS was outlawed under the terms of the Digital Millennium Copyright Act.

In November 2001, a federal appeals court reaffirmed the trial court decision in favor of the motion picture industry.[8] The court held that the DMCA is constitutional. It also said that Corley's posting of and linking to DeCSS was in direct violation of the anticircumvention provision of the DMCA. In May 2002 a court of appeals again upheld the ruling that the posting of and linking to DeCSS was in direct violation of the DMCA.

According to Jack Valenti, president and CEO of the MPAA,

> Three court rulings in a row have upheld the constitutionality of the DMCA and its application to the defendant's actions. The rulings are unambiguous and the message is clear: the DMCA is a viable and critical law that protects copyright holders from unauthorized abuse of their works in the digital arena.[9]

Russian Programmer Arrested for Allegedly Violating the DMCA. This case began in July 2001 when the Federal Bureau of Investigation (FBI) arrested Dmitry Sklyarov, a Russian programmer, at a conference in Las Vegas.[10] Sklyarov was the lead engineer on an ElcomSoft product known as the Advanced eBook Processor. This product allows people to copy electronic books and view them in other formats and on different computers.

Adobe Systems Inc. originally brought ElcomSoft's program to the FBI's attention. Adobe is a software company that produces an eBook Reader program designed to protect the content of an electronic book. They were concerned that Sklyarov's software allowed people to copy and view eBooks in other formats and on multiple computers.[11]

Later, Adobe withdrew its support for the criminal complaint against Sklyarov and recommended his release from federal custody. But Sklyarov was held in jail until August 6, 2001, when he was released on bail of $50,000, on the condition that he remain in Northern California.

On August 28, 2001, a grand jury indicted both Sklyarov and ElcomSoft for circumvention offenses under the DMCA. Under the charges, Sklyarov faced up to twenty-five years in prison and a fine of up to $2.25 million. ElcomSoft as a corporation faced a penalty of $2.5 million.

By December 2001, Sklyarov was released from U.S. custody and allowed to return home to Russia as part of an agreement. Under the agreement, Sklyarov had to testify for the United States government, which continued its case against his employer, ElcomSoft. As a result, all the charges against him would be dropped.[12]

In December 2002, a federal jury in San Jose, California, found ElcomSoft not guilty.[13] The court's decision cleared ElcomSoft of violating the DMCA.

Norwegian Teenager Accused of DVD Piracy. In January 2002, the Norwegian government charged teenager Jon Johansen—sometimes called "DVD Jon"—with allegedly creating software that breaks the encryption on DVDs and allows them to be copied.[14]

Johansen created the software called DeCSS in 1999 when he was just fifteen years old. In January 2000, Johansen won the Karoline Prize for his DeCSS software innovation. This national prize is awarded yearly to a Norwegian high school student with excellent grades who makes a significant contribution to society outside of school.

After the MPAA contacted Norwegian prosecutors, an indictment was brought. The MPAA requested a criminal investigation of the teen and his father, Per Johansen, who owned the equipment on which the DeCSS software was posted.[15]

Eventually Johansen was acquitted of the charges. However, Norwegian prosecutors announced in January 2003 that the decision would be appealed.[16] As a result, Johansen will be tried again for violating copyright laws.

RIAA v. *Verizon Internet Services.* The RIAA subpoenaed Verizon Internet Services in July 2002. The subpoena demanded that Verizon turn over the name of a subscriber who had downloaded six hundred songs from the Internet in one day.[17]

The RIAA was aware of the downloaded songs because people in the record industry visit online file-swapping services to spot illegal file trading.[18] Although the services do not display the users' names, they do show their Internet protocol (IP) addresses. An IP address is a set of digits that identify each user on the Internet. With the IP address, record companies can find out which Internet service provider the downloader is using. In this case the ISP was Verizon.[19]

In January 2003, a federal judge ruled in favor of the RIAA and said that under the DMCA, Verizon must turn over the name of the subscriber. The judge also said that the DMCA was intended to create a process for quickly identifying copyright infringement.[20]

The lawsuit was considered a key test of the DMCA. Under the DMCA, ISPs are protected from prosecution for their subscribers' actions as long as they turn over the name of the offender when subpoenaed.

Verizon won the case on appeal. The D.C. Circuit Court of Appeals found that the subpoenas were not authorized by the DMCA. Had Verizon lost, it and other ISPs would have had to provide their subscribers' names, addresses, and telephone numbers.

Critics of the original court decision were concerned about consumers' rights. For example, the Electronic Frontier Foundation (EFF) argued that the ruling gave consumers accused of copyright infringement fewer protections than someone charged with spreading lies about someone online. "The constitutional protection of Internet users is being compromised on the say-so of record labels without any court review whatsoever," says Fred von Lohmann, an EFF copyright attorney. "There's no need for them to go into court and have to make a showing that their case is legitimate. And that's entirely at odds with the way we treat other forms of unlawful speech."[21]

RIAA Sues Four College Students. In April 2003, the RIAA filed copyright infringement lawsuits against four college students.[22] They accused the students of setting up file-sharing services similar to Napster on their campus networks.

By using these Napster-like systems, students can share files on the college networks instead of using the Internet. In doing so, the downloads can take place much more quickly.

According to Cary Sherman, president of the RIAA,

> These systems are best described as "local area Napster networks." The court ruled that Napster was illegal and shut it down. These systems are just as illegal and operate in just the same manner. And just like Napster, they hurt artists, musicians, songwriters, those who invest in their work and the thousands of others who work to bring music to the public.[23]

One month after filing the lawsuit, the RIAA announced that it had reached out-of-court settlements with each of the students. Additionally, all the students were required to shut down their sites if they had not done so already.

The recording industry has pursued suits against hundreds of people who have downloaded music illegally, including college students.

The settlements range from $12,000 to $17,500 each and will be paid in installments over several years. Under the law, the minimum penalty per infringement is $750, and the maximum is $150,000.

Named in the suits were two students at Rensselaer Polytechnic Institute, one at Princeton, and one at Michigan Technological University.[24] The students also could face disciplinary action from their schools.

Sherman said that the RIAA will continue to investigate these types of services on college networks and that anyone with knowledge of such systems should report them to RIAA's music piracy hotline.

"We hope that these suits serve as a stiff deterrent to anyone who is operating or considering setting up a similar system," adds Sherman.[25]

RIAA Sues 261 Downloaders. In September 2003, the RIAA began "a wave of lawsuits," suing 261 people all over the country who it said had used p2p to distribute copyrighted music files. According to the RIAA, those sued had downloaded an average of one thousand songs each.[26]

Among those sued was Brianna LaHara, a twelve-year-old girl living in New York City. She and her family believed the downloading was legal because they had paid for the software that enabled them to use file-sharing services. When Brianna's mother agreed to apologize and pay $2,000, the RIAA dropped the suit.[27]

In addition, the RIAA announced an amnesty (forgiveness) program. Under the program, file-sharers would not be sued if they came forward and admitted their wrongdoing, deleted any copyrighted files, and promised not to do it again.[28]

Other Lawsuits

There are numerous lawsuits surrounding copyright and peer-to-peer file sharing. Here are some additional lawsuits that were not yet decided at the time of publication:

- RIAA and MPAA sue MusicCity (now Streamcast) and Grokster. Both Streamcast and Grokster are programs that share files.

- RIAA clashes with Kazaa. Kazaa is a file-sharing service that is extremely popular for sharing music and movies.

- RIAA targets 754 individual file sharers. Lawsuits were filed in Pennsylvania, Virginia, Georgia, Missouri, New York, Connecticut, Illinois, and the District of Columbia. Users of university computer networks made up a portion of these lawsuits.

What's Next? The Future of the Underground Internet

Much of the battle over copyright and peer-to-peer technology boils down to a "leave it alone" versus "shut it down or control it" argument. Both sides agree that piracy is wrong and that peer-to-peer technology is here to stay. They do not agree on how piracy should be prevented. Nor do they agree on how the technology should be used in the process.

Copyright owners want to be able to fight piracy and protect their work using current laws, educational efforts, digital rights management, and the self-help measures proposed in the P2P Piracy Prevention Act. The opposition, such as the EFF, EPIC, and similar organizations, wants to be sure consumers' rights are not trampled in the process. Although they agree that piracy is wrong and that creators deserve to be paid, they also stress the importance of free speech, fair use, privacy, and research. They argue that while fighting copyright infringement is important, the rights of the public should not be infringed upon either.

Because the battle is so new, it is hard to say how it will play out in the courts and in Congress. As legal battles are decided and as Congress revises and passes legislation, the groundwork will be laid for the futures of both copyrights and peer-to-peer technology.

In the meantime, the copyright industries, particularly the music industry, are taking steps to change and to better meet their customers' needs. For example, record labels have started to develop relationships with online music stores. These stores allow music fans to download music from the Internet—and the artists are paid, too. Second, the music industry is starting to get creative so that they can still sell CDs.

Online Music Stores

In response to consumer demand to get their music online, two companies began offering music downloading services in 2003. Through these services, music lovers now can pay per song, or subscribe and get unlimited music. Both services are legal downloading options and are supported by the recording industry.

The first company to really get the ball rolling was Apple, which launched the iTunes Music Store in April 2003. At its debut, iTunes featured a catalog of more than 200,000 songs from music companies including BMG, EMI, Sony Music Entertainment, Universal, and Warner.[1] By October 2003, the company reported more than 14 million downloads since it launched and had increased the number of songs available to 400,000.[2]

Steve Jobs, Apple's CEO, says:

The iTunes Music Store offers the revolutionary rights to burn an unlimited number of CDs for personal use and to put music on an unlimited number of iPods for on-the-go listening. Consumers don't want to be treated like criminals and artists don't want their valuable work stolen. The iTunes Music Store offers a groundbreaking solution for both.[3]

In addition to burning songs onto unlimited CDs, users can play songs on up to three computers. They can also listen to a free 30-second preview of any song in the store.

According to Dylan (not his real name), a music lover and an employee of a software development company, Apple's solution to getting music online is a better choice than the sites that offer free file sharing.

"I never used Napster [when it was free] despite loving music . . . because I like my music to sound great and MP3s often aren't ripped at a high enough bit rate to satisfy me," Dylan explains. By contrast, the songs he has downloaded from iTunes are of high quality.[4]

Dylan says he has created a music library of more than 1,600 songs. Although most of his library is from CDs he already owns, he has added to his collection with the iTunes Music Store. According to Dylan,

Being able to spend $15 and get fifteen great tunes is better than buying a single CD with two great tunes. [Plus] with the iPod and burning capabilities of the computer, I can tote all my favorite music wherever I go. I can hook my iPod up to my buddy's stereo and we can listen to all the cool music I have collected.[5]

Dylan says he also likes the exclusive tracks where featured artists provide different versions of their songs. As a result, he has purchased quite a few of those. He says the music store also recommends other artists based on his choices. Dylan says:

I find myself buying other artists I wouldn't have even considered in a physical music store. What I have been doing lately is listening

By subscribing to legal music downloading services, people can download the music they like and enjoy it without cheating the artists.

to an Internet radio station during the day [Radio Paradise in California] and keeping a list of cool music I hear. When I find one of them on iTunes I buy it. To date, I have bought sixty-three songs from the iTunes Music Store—equivalent to buying only four CDs at $15 a pop. The difference is that I love every tune I bought from iTunes.[6]

Initially, Apple's software was available to only Mac users. Then, in October 2003, Apple launched a Windows version of the software. They also incorporated features that allow for buying and sending gift certificates and setting up "allowance" accounts for children whose parents do not want to give them access to a credit card number.[7]

Also in October 2003, Napster, now owned by Roxio, returned to the downloading scene with a legal version of its service called Napster 2.0. Like Apple, Napster users can purchase individual songs for just 99 cents or subscribe and get unlimited music. In addition, Napster claims to have the world's largest collection of music available, with more than 500,000 songs.[8]

"We have created the most exciting and comprehensive music experience in the world," Chris Gorog, chairman and CEO, says. "Napster 2.0 is extremely easy to use and music fans will find endless enjoyment as they search for, discover and share music."[9]

The new service will feature exclusive tracks and live sessions recorded in Napster's Los Angeles studio from Guided By Voices, MxPx, Brian McKnight, and Cold, among others.

For years music fans have been asking for a legal online music alternative where they can share and discover music and pay as they go, says Dylan. Now they have what they want. He continues:

I believe using free file-sharing services is certainly wrong, [but] in the case of the music industry, I believe they needed a big wake-up call. The Internet allows me to listen to a radio station in California, without commercials. [And], paying 99 cents for a song

I love is a no-brainer. My appetite for music is no different than it was in the past. The difference now is that I can be much more selective and also take more risks because it only costs me 99 cents![10]

As a whole, online music sales are expected to grow from 1 percent of the total music market to 12 percent in 2008, according to Jupiter Research. This increase will generate about $1.5 billion in sales, they say.[11]

A New Way to Sell CDs

Faced with the fact that online file sharing cuts into CD sales, Jon Bon Jovi released his latest album with some interesting incentives for buyers. The record company, Island Records, is giving consumers a good reason—other than the music—to buy the CD. Each album has a unique PIN code that allows the buyer to register online and gain the right to some exclusive opportunities on an ongoing basis.[12]

People who buy the album get first rights to concert tickets and even some opportunities to go onstage. They also get exclusive chats with the band, contests for trips and merchandise, and special performances streamed on the Internet.[13]

Piracy Is Unethical

Both sides agree that piracy is unethical. It is wrong to steal. Even though you may be in the privacy of your own home downloading free files, it is still very much like snatching CDs, DVDs, and computer games off the shelves of your local store and stuffing them into your bag, pockets, or pants. The creators of those items spent a lot of time, energy, and money developing those products, and they deserve to be paid for their efforts.

Unfortunately, though, piracy on the Internet will always exist to some extent. Every time an organization like the Recording Industry Association of America shuts down a file-sharing organization, more will pop up to take its place.

That does not mean that people have to help this illegal underground world of free stuff survive.

Here are some reasons why people should think twice before downloading free copyrighted material:

- Pirating copyrighted material such music, movies, and software is against the law. Creative people have the right to be paid for their work. The law gives them the right to authorize—or not to authorize—copies of their work. Unauthorized copying—meaning you do not have permission from the copyright holder—is against the law, and the penalties for breaking the law are high. For example, you could spend up to five years in prison and owe $250,000 in fines.

- Pirating copyrighted material hurts the people who created it. Many people who illegally download or share files believe they are not hurting anyone. After all, they reason, "They're all rich anyway, right?" Not so. Artists and creators have to pay their bills just like anyone else. They deserve to get paid for their work—just like you deserve a paycheck for the work you do.

- Pirating copyrighted material can damage the careers of new artists. One popular argument for peer-to-peer file sharing is that unsigned artists could use it as a tool. Sure, it could be used that way. But the whole reason many artists would use the technology is to build an audience and "get noticed" by a record company. Unfortunately, though, if the record companies are being ripped off, there will not be any money to pick up those new artists, no matter how good they are.

- Pirating copyrighted material puts the jobs of people employed by the copyright industries at risk. In 2001, the copyright industries employed 4.7 million workers. These workers included everyone from management employees and creators to technicians, plant workers, and warehouse employees. By stealing copyrighted material, you are putting the jobs of millions of people in jeopardy.[14]

Help Prevent Online Piracy

So, what can you do to help? Start by using legal ways to get music, movies, and software. For example, you could use online stores or subscription services such as iTunes, Napster 2.0, or Music Match to download music.

Secondly, check out the antipiracy sections of the Web sites of the Recording Industry Association of America (RIAA), the Motion Picture Association of America (MPAA), and the Software Information Industry Association (SIIA). By doing so you will be able to see where the copyright industries stand on piracy.

Thirdly, make sure your friends know what is legal and what is not—and what can happen to them if they do pirate material. When you know piracy is taking place, report it.

To report suspected music piracy, contact the RIAA. You can make a complaint by telephone or by e-mail. For suspected movie and video piracy, contact the MPAA. You can make a complaint by telephone or by e-mail.

Finally, if you suspect software piracy, you can contact the Business Software Alliance (BSA) or the SIIA.

The Potential of Peer-to-Peer Technology

Remember that peer-to-peer technology does not always equal piracy. Sure, peer-to-peer file sharing has been used mostly for less than upstanding purposes such as pirating copies of music, movies, and software. As a result, a number of powerful organizations have an extremely negative opinion of peer-to-peer technology—mainly because it has been used to rip them off.

Because there are so many positive aspects to this technology, not everyone sees peer-to-peer simply as a piracy tool. While the full potential of peer-to-peer technology has yet to be realized, there are hints of interest in this technology. The Gartner Group says that 30 percent of all United States corporations had experimented with peer-to-peer technology by the end of 2003.[15]

Peer-to-peer networks allow large numbers of people to exchange information and ideas in new and exciting ways, and it is not terribly expensive to develop. Overall, peer-to-peer's potential for use in organizing, promoting, and sharing information is huge.

Consequently, a number of organizations are hoping to succeed by using the same technology. Both businesspeople and the military are interested. They want to use peer-to-peer technology to help people to be more efficient and creative and to solve communication problems.

How the Military Is Using P2P

Peer-to-peer is particularly popular with the military—especially when fighting terrorism and wars abroad, such as the 2003 war with Iraq. With a program similar to Napster, military planning is easier. Small units can communicate with each other without going up and down the chain of command.

Unfortunately, adversaries of the United States have also benefited from Internet-style networks. For example, al Qaeda is a widely distributed network, which makes it difficult to destroy. Some experts say that it would help if our military strategies were decentralized.[16]

One company the military is using is Groove Networks, which makes peer-to-peer software. Using the program Groove Workspace, which is installed on a laptop computer, naval physician Commander Eric Rasmussen can handle a number of tasks while in the field.[17] For example, he can alert others to incidents that could affect them as well as make casualty reports and evacuation requests. By using his computer, he no longer has to carry around field radios, pagers, phones, and other communication gear.

The Groove program is extremely secure. Messages shared with others are automatically ultra-encrypted, which makes them very difficult to crack.[18] The information is shared by others on the team. If his laptop stops working because of a sandstorm or some other reason, Rasmussen just contacts one of the other "shared space" members and installs a copy on a fresh computer.

How Businesses Are Using P2P

Businesses also are taking an interest in peer-to-peer technology—especially large companies with offices in different cities. Many times workers duplicate letters, reports, or proposals because they do not realize that the same thing already exists someplace else. Using peer-to-peer technology, they are better able to share ideas and information. By sharing information, they can avoid recreating something already in existence.

In business today, important information is often stored in different locations. As a result, companies do not always have a clear understanding of what information is available. Companies also have difficulty connecting the right people with the right expertise to make decisions and complete projects efficiently.[19] This technology allows users to simultaneously access resources and information as if they existed in a single location.

For example, the law firm Baker and McKenzie uses a peer-to-peer program developed by the company NextPage. As a result, the attorneys in the firm's sixty-one offices can access files on one another's hard drives and work together on legal documents.[20]

"The [NextPage] system connects attorneys to all the relevant information and people required to complete a transaction—saving time and improving the decision-making process," says

Businesses are starting to use p2p technology to link people working in different locations.

Mark Swords, an international partner for Baker and McKenzie. "This capability further enhances the service we provide to the client—a significant competitive advantage for our firm."[21]

Overall, peer-to-peer technology presents one of the biggest opportunities—and challenges—ever. Napster proved that peer-to-peer works. Now sharing information and files is no longer limited to a few friends copying software, a movie, or a CD among themselves. The entire population of Internet users can share any digital file anytime. Despite its messy history, it is obvious that file sharing is changing the Internet.

Chapter Notes

Chapter 1 Downloading: A History

1. Interview with college student (real name withheld), January 2003.
2. Mary Madden and Amanda Lenhart, "Music Downloading, File-Sharing and Copyright," Pew Internet & American Life Project, July 2003, <http://www.pewinternet.org/reports/pdfs/PIP_Copyright_Memo.pdf> (April 6, 2004).
3. Ibid.
4. Interview with college student (real name withheld).
5. Pew Internet & American Life Project, "Pew Internet Project Survey Shows 13 Million Music 'Freeloaders' on Internet; 1 Billion Free Music Files Among Napster Users," press release, June 8, 2000, <http://www.pewinternet.org> (March 19, 2003).
6. "Report: Napster Users Lose That Sharing Feeling," *CNN.com*, June 28, 2001, <http://www.cnn.com/2001/TECH/internet/06/28/napster.usage> (May 8, 2003).
7. Christos J.P. Moschovitis et al., "History of the Internet," 1999, <http://www.historyoftheinternet.com/chap3.html> (April 6, 2004).
8. Ibid.
9. David E. Carlson, "Bulletin Board Systems," 1998–2002, <http://iml.jou.ufl.edu/carlson/profession/new_media/history/bbs.htm> (February 2, 2003).
10. Hilary Rosen, "Peer-to-Peer Piracy on University Campuses," Statement before the United States House of Representatives, February 26, 2003, <http://www.riaa.com/news/newsletter/022603.asp> (March 25, 2004).
11. Ibid.
12. Recording Industry Association of America, "Music Community Steps Up Educational Efforts, Communicates Directly With P2P Users," press release, April 29, 2003, <http://www.riaa.com/PR_Story.cfm?id=634> (May 24, 2003).
13. Ibid.
14. Ibid.

Chapter 2 Tools of the Underground Internet

1. Warren Cohen, "Napster is Rocking the Music Industry," *U.S. News & World Report*, vol. 128, no. 9, March 6, 2000, p. 41.
2. Ibid.

3. "Metallica Fingers 300,000 Napster Users," *TechWeb,* May 2, 2000.

4. Melissa Blazek, "A Napster Timeline," *Grammy.com,* February 23, 2003, <http://grammy.aol.com/features/0130_naptimeline.html> (March 20, 2003).

5. Roxio, Inc., "Roxio Acquires PressPlay as the Foundation for the Re-Launch of Napster," press release, May 19, 2003.

6. Ibid.

7. Peter J. Gordon, interview with the author, January 2003.

8. Chris Dahlen, "How to Survive Without Audiogalaxy: A Guide to File-Sharing Alternatives," June 27, 2002, <http://www.pitchfork media.com/watw/02–06/audiogalaxy.shtml> (March 25, 2004).

9. "WinMX," *PC Magazine,* March 12, 2002.

10. "What is Freenet?" *The Free Network Project,* n.d., <http://freenet project.org/index.php?page=faq> (February 27, 2003).

11. Ibid.

Chapter 3   The Underground Internet Today

1. Colin Gabriel Hatcher, "Why You Should Care About Downloading Pirate Software, Movies and Music," 2001, <http://www.safetyed.org/help/pirate. html> (March 25, 2002).

2. Ipsos–Reid, "Legal Issues Don't Hinder American Downloaders," press release, March 14, 2003, <http://www.ipsosreid.com/media/dsp_ displaypr_us.cfm?id_to_view=1763> (March 23, 2003).

3. "The Economic Picture," Motion Picture Association of America, March 26, 2002, <http://www.mpaa.org/anti-piracy> (March 25, 2004).

4. "The Effects of Piracy," Recording Industry Association of America, n.d., <http://www.riaa.com/Protect–Campaign–3.cfm> (May 25, 2003).

5. "The Economic Picture."

6. "Software Piracy Fact Sheet," Business Software Alliance, March 26, 2002.

7. Hatcher.

8. Ibid.

9. "The No Electronic Theft (NET) Act," January 2003, <http://www.cyber crime.gov/netsum.htm> (May 8, 2003).

10. "United States of America v. David LaMacchia," January 2003, <http:// www.loundy.com/CASES/US_v_LaMacchia.html> (May 25, 2003).

11. "The No Electronic Theft (NET) Act."

12. "Digital Millennium Copyright Act," n.d., <http://webopedia.com/ TERM/D/DMCA.html> (March 29, 2003).

13. "World Intellectual Property Organization," *Wikipedia,* n.d., <http://www. wikipedia.org/wiki/World_Intellectual_Property_Organization> (March 30, 2003).

14. "Berne Convention for the Protection of Literary and Artistic Works," *Wikipedia,* n.d., <http://www.wikipedia.org/wiki/Berne_Convention_for_ the_Protection_of_Literary_and_Artistic_Works> (March 30, 2003).

15. Ibid.

16. Ibid.

17. "Agreement on Trade-Related Aspects of Intellectual Property Rights," *Wikipedia,* n.d., <http://www.wikipedia.org/wiki/Trade_Related_aspects_ of_Intellectual_Property_rights> (March 30, 2003).

18. McGregor McCance, "Congress Takes Up Internet File-Swapping Issue," *Knight Ridder/Tribune Business News,* January 12, 2003.

19. "Beyond the Music: Peer-to-Peer File-Sharing Web Sites Grow 300 Percent, Driven by Swapping Movies, Games and More, Reports Websense Inc.," press release, *Websense,* January 23, 2003, <http://www. websense.com/company/news/pr/Display.php?Release=03012359> (March 25, 2004).

20. Ibid.

21. Ibid.

22. Conor Dougherty, "Fighting the Rising Swapping Tide," *Los Angeles Business Journal,* vol. 25, no. 4, January 27, 2003, p. 1.

Chapter 4   Free Speech? The Argument for
the Underground Internet

1. Nelson Minar and Marc Hedlund, "A Network of Peers," *Peer-to-Peer: Harnessing the Power of Disruptive Technologies,* March 2001, <http://www. oreilly.com/catalog/peertopeer/chapter/ch01.html> (March 29, 2003).

2. Deidre Mulligan, Nicky Ozer and Nicolai Nelson, "Unintended Consequences: Four Years under the DMCA," Electronic Frontier Foundation, 2003, <http://www.eff.org/IP/DMCA/20030102_dmca_ unintended_consequences.html> (March 29, 2003).

3. "Campaign for Audiovisual Free Expression (CAFE)," Electronic Frontier Foundation, n.d., <http://www.eff.org/cafe/indexcenter2.html> (March 29, 2003).

4. Forrester Research, "Downloads Did Not Cause the Music Slump, But They Can Cure It," press release, August 13, 2002, <http://www.forrester. com/ER/Press/Release/0,1769,741,00.html> (December 30, 2004).

5. Interview with software developer (name withheld), October 2003.

6. Forrester Research.

7. Ibid.

8. Ibid.

9. "Court Decision on DMCA Subpoenas Raises Privacy Issues; Law Must Balance Copyright Enforcement with Privacy, Free Expression," Statement by the Center of Democracy & Technology, January 30, 2003, <http://www.cdt.org/copyright/030130cdt.shtml> (April 1, 2003).

10. Public Knowledge, "Gigi B. Sohn, President, Public Knowledge, Testifies on 'Piracy of Intellectual Property on Peer-to-Peer Networks' Before the House Judiciary Subcommittee on the Courts, the Internet and Intellectual Property," press release, September 26, 2002, <http://www.publicknowledge.org/content/press-releases/press-release–gigi–testifies> (March 25, 2004).

11. Mark Anderson, "A Cold Look At Chilled Speech," *Wired News,* October 3, 2001, <http://www.wired.com/news/privacy/0,1848,47195,00.html> (March 25, 2004).

12. Electronic Frontier Foundation, "Princeton Scientists Sue over Squelched Research: Electronic Frontier Foundation Challenges Record Companies," press release, June 6, 2001, <http://www.eff.org/Legal/Cases/Felten_v_RIAA/20010606_eff_felten_pr.html> (March 25, 2004).

13. Ibid.

14. Mulligan, Ozer, and Nelson.

15. Ibid.

16. Ibid.

17. Ibid.

18. "EPIC Digital Rights Management and Privacy Page," Electronic Privacy Information Center, n.d., <http://www.epic.org/privacy/drm> (April 11, 2003).

19. Ibid.

20. Ibid.

21. Ibid.

22. Mulligan, Ozer, and Nelson.

23. Ibid.

24. Representative Rick Boucher, "Digital Media Consumers' Rights Act," n.d., <http://www.house.gov/boucher/docs/dmcrahandout.htm> (April 8, 2003).

25. "Empower Consumers and Everybody Wins," Statement of Representative Rick Boucher Before the Harvard Journal of Law and Technology Symposium: Copyright and Fair Use: The Present and Future Perspective,

March 15, 2003, <http://www.house.gov/boucher/docs/harvard.htm> (April 8, 2003).

26. Interview with college graduate (real name withheld), November 2003.

27. Ibid.

28. "Company Information and Testimonials," *Garageband.com,* November 2003, <http://www.garageband.com/htdb/companyinfo/testimonials.html> (November 4, 2003).

29. Ibid.

30. Joseph Szadkowski, "Music Gets on the Net," *Insight on the News,* vol. 15, no. 47, December 20, 1999, p. 32.

31. Interview with college graduate.

Chapter 5 Copyright Infringement? The Argument Against the Underground Internet

1. "The Effects of Piracy," Recording Industry Association of America, n.d., <http://www.riaa.org/Protect–Campaign–3.cfm> (March 29, 2003).

2. "Anti-Piracy: The Economic Picture," Motion Picture Association of America, n.d., <http://www.mpaa.org/anti-piracy> (March 26, 2002).

3. "How Piracy Impacts You," Microsoft Piracy Basics, n.d., <http://www.microsoft.com/piracy/basics/how> (April 2, 2003).

4. Peter Chernin, "The Problem with Stealing," Comdex Fall 2002 Keynote Speaker, November 19, 2002, <http://www.copyrightassembly.org/briefing/test_2002_11_19.htm> (March 26, 2004).

5. Copyright Assembly, "Copyright Facts," 2002, <http://www.copyrightassembly.org/facts/default.htm> (April 5, 2003).

6. Copyright Assembly, "Our Perspective," 2002, <http://www.copyrightassembly.org/perspective/default.htm> (April 5, 2003).

7. Chernin.

8. Conor Dougherty, "Fighting the Rising Swapping Tide," *Los Angeles Business Journal,* vol. 25, no. 4, January 27, 2003, p. 1.

9. Copyright Assembly, "Our Perspective."

10. California Senate Testimony of Matthew J. Oppenheim, Vice President, Business and Legal Affairs, Recording Industry Association of America, March 27, 2003, <http://www.riaa.com/news/newsletter/032703_testimony.asp> (March 26, 2004).

11. Ibid.

12. Ibid.

13. Minority Staff Special Investigations Division Committee on Government Reform, "Children's Access to Pornography Through Internet File-Sharing Programs," U.S. House of Representatives, July 27, 2001.

14. Ibid.

15. Interview with Internet marketing agency employee (real name withheld), October 2003.

16. Motion Picture Association of America, "Study Shows Copyright Industries as Largest Contributor to the U.S. Economy," press release, April 22, 2002, <http://www.mpaa.org/copyright/2002_04_22.htm> (March 26, 2003).

17. Ibid.

18. Robert Holleyman, "If Content is Pirated, Eventually it Vanishes," *Mercury News,* May 20, 2002, <http://www.bayarea.com/mld/mercurynews/news/opinion/3299375.htm> (April 5, 2003).

19. Susan J. Marks, "Digital Rights Management and the Bottom Line," *CIO Insight,* October 10, 2002, <http://www.cioinsight.com/article2/0,1397,1458938,00.asp> (April 10, 2003).

20. Ibid.

Chapter 6 Underground Internet Lawsuits and Their Outcomes

1. "A Radical Rethink: Copyrights," *The Economist,* vol. 366, no. 8308, January 25, 2003.

2. Melissa Blazek, "A Napster Timeline," *Grammy.com,* February 23, 2003, <http://www.grammy.aol.com/features/0130_naptimeline.html> (March 20, 2003).

3. "Roxio Buys Napster's Name and Patents," *Internet Business News,* November 29, 2002.

4. Erik Gruenwedel, "Court OK's Napster Asset Sale to Roxio," *Billboard Bulletin,* December 2, 2002, p. 1.

5. Brian Garrity, "Roxio in Talks with Majors for New Napster Service," *Billboard Bulletin,* February 20, 2003, p. 1.

6. "Beyond the Music: Peer-to-Peer File-Sharing Web Sites Grow 300 Percent, Driven by Swapping Movies, Games and More, Reports Websense Inc.," press release, *Websense,* January 23, 2003, <http://www.websense.com/company/news/pr/Display.php?Release=03012359> (March 25, 2004).

7. "Kaplan Issues Ruling in New York DeCSS Case," *Digital Copyright Court Cases,* <http://www.acm.org/usacm/copyright/dmca.htm> (April 22, 2003).

8. Motion Picture Association of America, "MPAA's Valenti Applauds New York Appeals Court Ruling Upholding Lower Court Decision in Motion Picture Industry DeCSS Case," press release, November 29, 2002, <http://www.mpaa.org/press/2001_11_29.htm> (May 22, 2003).

9. Motion Picture Association of America, "MPAA's Valenti Applauds New York Second Circuit Court of Appeals Decision to Uphold Lower Court Decision in Motion Picture Industry DeCSS Case," press release, May 17, 2002, <http://www.mpaa.org/press/2002_05_17a.htm> (May 22, 2003).

10. Electronic Frontier Foundation, "Jury Acquits ElcomSoft in eBook Copyright Case," press release, December 17, 2002, <http://www.eff.org/IP/DMCA/US_v_Elcomsoft/20021217_eff_pr.html> (May 16, 2003).

11. Electronic Frontier Foundation, "What Is Adobe's Role in this Case?" *U.S. v. ElcomSoft & Sklyarov FAQ*, February 19, 2002, <http://www.eff.org/IP/DMCA/US_v_Elcomsoft/us_v_elcomsoft_faq.html#AdobeRole> (March 26, 2004).

12. Electronic Frontier Foundation, "What Is the History and Current Status of this Case?" *U.S. v. ElcomSoft & Sklyarov FAQ*, February 19, 2002, <http://www.eff.org/IP/DMCA/US_v_Elcomsoft/us_v_elcomsoft_faq.html#Status> (May 16, 2003).

13. Electronic Frontier Foundation, "Jury Acquits ElcomSoft in eBook Copyright Case."

14. Electronic Frontier Foundation, "Norway Indicts Teen Who Published Code Liberating DVDs," press release, January 10, 2002, <http://www.eff.org/IP/Video/DeCSS_prosecutions/Johansen_DeCSS_case/20020110_eff_pr.html> (May 16, 2003).

15. Ibid.

16. "Norwegian DVD Piracy Case Acquittal Appealed," *The Online Reporter,* January 25, 2003.

17. Dawn C. Chmielewksi, "Verizon Ordered to Name Subscriber," *Mercury News,* January 22, 2003, <http://www.mercurynews.com/mld/mercurynews/business/5003250.htm> (March 26, 2004).

18. Hiawatha Bray, "Federal Court Rules Verizon Must Reveal Identity of Internet Subscriber," *Boston Globe* (Knight Ridder/Tribune Business News), January 22, 2003.

19. Ibid.

20. Chmielewski.

21. Ibid.

22. Dawn C. Chmielewski, "Recording Industry Sues Four College Students Over File-Swapping," *UGAToday.com,* April 14, 2003, <http://www.uga today.com/vnews/display.v?TARGET=printable&article_id=3e9abf32cfea7> (April 22, 2003).

23. Recording Industry Association of America, "RIAA Moves Against Operators of P2P Systems Housed on Internal College Networks," press release, April 2003, <http://www.riaa.com/news/newsletters/040303_2.asp> (May 21, 2003).

24. Bill Holland, "RIAA Settles with Students," *Billboard Bulletin,* May 2, 2003, p. 1.

25. Recording Industry Association of America.

26. Katie Dean, "RIAA Legal Landslide Begins," *Wired News,* September 8, 2003, <http://www.wired.com/news/digiwood/0,1412,60345,00.html> (April 7, 2004).

27. Ted Bridis, "Music Industry Settles Suit Against New York Girl, 12," *Salt Lake Tribune,* September 10, 2003, <http://www.sltrib.com/2003/Sep/09102003/nation/_w91260.asp> (April 7, 2004).

28. Dean.

Chapter 7   What's Next? The Future of the Underground Internet

1. Apple Computers, "Apple Launches the iTunes Music Store," press release, April 28, 2003, <http://www.apple.com/pr/library/2003/apr/28music store.html> (October 30, 2003).

2. "Launch Day for 'Legitimate' Napster," *BBC News,* October 30, 2003.

3. Apple Computers.

4. Interview with employee of software development company (real name withheld), October 2003.

5. Ibid.

6. Ibid.

7. "Apple has sold 1 million songs on iTunes for Windows," *Reuters,* October 21, 2003, <http://in.tech.yahoo.com/031021/137/28o7q.html> (October 20, 2004).

8. Roxio, Inc., "Napster's Back," press release, October 29, 2003.

9. Ibid.

10. Interview with employee of software development company.

11. "Launch Day for 'Legitimate' Napster."

12. Michael J. Dolan, "Napster Just the Start of Rights Fight," *Daily Variety,* vol. 278, no. 43, March 5, 2003, p. 36.
13. Ibid.
14. Suki Shergill-Connolly, "Explain the Legal Consequences of Pirating Music," March 12, 2003, <http://www.connectingwithkids.com/tipsheet/2003/115_mar12/music.html> (April 14, 2003).
15. Julie Schlosser, "Sharing," *Fortune,* vol. 143, no. 13, June 25, 2001, p. 156.
16. D. C. Denison, "Military Mind-Set Continues to Hatch Internet Ideas," *Boston Globe,* April 6, 2003, p. H2.
17. "Commander Eric Rasmussen, U.S. Navy Case Study," *Groove Networks,* February 24, 2003, <http://www.groove.net/default.cfm?pagename=Case Study_Rasmussen> (April 8, 2003).
18. Ibid.
19. "Company Backgrounder," NEXTPage Press Kit, 2003, <http://www.nextpage.com/news/presskit/companybackground.htm> (April 8, 2003).
20. Schlosser.
21. "Quotes from Industry Analysts and NEXTPage Customers," 2003, NEXTPage Press Kit, <http://www.nextpage.com/news/presskit/quotes.htm> (April 8, 2003).

Glossary

application—Any program designed to perform a specific function.

centralized—Technology that uses a central server.

circumvention device—A method used to break copy protection on DVDs. This practice makes it possible for movies on DVDs to be decrypted.

client—Someone who requests information from a file-sharing service.

copyright—A form of protection provided by the laws of the United States to the person or organization that created the material.

cracker—A computer programmer who breaks the protection codes on software. The software posted online is called a "cracked" copy.

decentralized—Technology that does not have a central server.

DeCSS—Software that copies an encrypted DVD file and saves the file on a hard disk minus the encryption.

digital rights management (DRM)—Copy-protection devices that provide security for copyrighted materials by controlling how many times and how long you can look at something. It can also control sharing, copying, changing, printing, and saving.

digital watermarking—Software that allows copyright owners to insert a digital stamp into their data that acts as a copyright statement and travels with the material throughout its use.

encrypt—To change material into a format that is not easily understood by unauthorized people.

encryption envelope—Software that creates a "secure container" around the material that keeps the content away from other people while in the user's hands and prevents the material from being changed.

fair use—A limitation on copyright that allows the public to use copyrighted work without having to ask permission, as long as the use does not interfere with the copyright owner's market for the work.

file-sharing network protocol—A standard way for file-sharing services to communicate or work.

file-sharing services—Software applications or programs designed to perform a specific job.

filters—Software programs usually installed on computers to limit the types of material that can be viewed.

indict—To charge with an offense or a crime.

intellectual property—Any product that has been created by someone and has value in the marketplace. Some examples include a computer program process, a unique name, or an invention.

Internet—A massive network that connects millions of computers together around the world.

Internet protocol (IP) address—A set of digits that identifies each user on the Internet.

MP3 (MPEG-1 Layer 3)—An MP3 is a digital format that allows people to compress music files without affecting the quality of sound.

peer—A device such as a PC, sometimes called a node, that is able to make requests and to accept requests started someplace else.

peer-to-peer (p2p)—Technology that allows two or more devices, such as personal computers, to share files and information through the Internet.

pirate—(v) To make copies of copyrighted material without permission from the owner or copyright holder; (n) person who makes copies of copyrighted material without permission from the owner or copyright holder.

pornography—Inappropriate sexually explicit material.

protocol—Language used for information to travel over the Internet.

reverse engineering—Taking apart an object to see how it works in order to duplicate or enhance the object.

servent—Someone who acts as a server (providing information) and a client (requesting information) at the same time.

server—Someone who offers information in a file-sharing environment.

shareware—Software that is distributed free on a trial basis with the understanding that if the user decides he needs it later he will pay for it.

spyware—A program that secretly collects information on what users are doing on their PCs.

super nodes—Powerful PCs that have fast connections to the Internet. They are identified by the p2p system to devote a small percentage of their resources to help run the network.

warez—A slang term for pirated software or software that is copied without permission.

World Wide Web—A way of accessing information over the Internet. It is an information-sharing model that is built on top of the Internet.

For More Information

Business Software Alliance (BSA) United States
1150 18th Street NW
Suite 700
Washington, DC 20036
(202) 872–5500

Center for Democracy and Technology
1634 Eye Street NW, Suite 1100
Washington, DC 20006
(202) 637–9800

Digital Future Coalition
1341 G Street NW, Suite 200
Washington, DC 20005
(202) 628–9210

Electronic Privacy Information Center (EPIC)
1718 Connecticut Avenue NW
Suite 200
Washington, DC 20009
(202) 483–1140

Entertainment Software Association
12 Connecticut Avenue NW, #600
Washington, DC 20036

Future of Music Coalition
c/o Michael Bracy
1615 L Street NW, Suite 520
Washington, DC 20036
(202) 429–8855

Motion Picture Association of America (MPAA)
15503 Ventura Blvd.
Encino, CA 91436
(818) 995–6600

Privacy Foundation
Mary Reed Building
2199 S. University Blvd.
Denver, CO 80208
(303) 871–4971

Public Knowledge
1875 Connecticut Avenue NW
Suite 650
Washington, DC 20009
(202) 518–0020

The Software & Information Industry Association.
1090 Vermont Avenue NW
Sixth Floor
Washington, DC 20005
(202) 289–7442

U.S. Copyright Office
101 Independence Avenue SE
Washington, DC 20559–6000
(202) 707–3000

U.S. Department of Justice
10th & Constitution Avenue NW
Criminal Division (Computer Crime & Intellectual Property Section)
John C. Keeney Building, Suite 600
Washington, DC 20530
(202) 514–1026

Further Reading

Books

Craig, Tom. *Internet: Technology, People, Process.* North Mankato, Minn.: Smart Apple Media, 2003.

Menhard, Francha Roffé. *Internet Issues: Pirates, Censors, and Cybersquatters.* Berkeley Heights, N.J.: Enslow Publishers, Inc., 2001.

Mitten, Christopher. *Shawn Fanning: Napster and the Music Revolution.* Brookfield, Conn.: Twenty-first Century Books, 2002.

Sherman, Josepha. *The History of the Internet.* New York: Franklin Watts, 2003.

Stoyles, Pennie, Peter Pentland, and David Demant. *Information Technology.* North Mankato, Minn.: Smart Apple Media, 2003.

Wolinsky, Art. *Safe Surfing on the Internet.* Berkeley Heights, N.J.: Enslow Publishers, Inc., 2003.

Internet Addresses

Electronic Frontier Foundation
<http://www.eff.org>

Recording Industry Association of America
<http://www.riaa.com>

U.S. Copyright Office Home Page
<http://lcweb.loc.gov/copyright/>

Index